THE NIGHT COUNTRY

∧∧∧∧∧∧∧∧∧∧∧∧∧∧∧∧∧∧∧∧∧∧∧∧∧∧∧∧∧∧∧∧∧

LOREN EISELEY

THE
NIGHT
COUNTRY

CHARLES SCRIBNER'S SONS   NEW YORK

AMERICAN MUSEUM OF NATURAL HISTORY
SPECIAL MEMBERS EDITION

IN MEMORY OF MY GRANDMOTHER
Malvina McKee Corey
1850-1936
WHO SLEEPS AS ALL MY PEOPLE SLEEP
BY THE WAYS OF THE WESTWARD CROSSING

CONTENTS ·

FOREWORD

Last week, scuffing the turf while waiting for a plane flight to begin, I turned up a broken wheel from a child's toy. It had once been painted a golden yellow. On impulse I pushed it into the pocket of my topcoat. "For luck," I said to myself and shivered. My mind ran instantly back along a dimension hazy even to myself.

This volume, as all my readers will recognize, has been drawn from many times and places in the wilderness of a single life. Though I sit in a warm room beneath a lamp as I arrange these pieces, my thoughts are all of night, of outer cold and inner darkness. These chapters, then, are the annals of a long and uncompleted running. I leave them here lest the end come on me unawares as it does upon all fugitives.

There is a shadow on the wall before me. It is my own; the hour is late. I write in a hotel room at midnight. Tomorrow the shadow on the wall will be that of another.

LOREN EISELEY

1

THE GOLD WHEEL

I

IN the waste fields strung with barbed wire where the thistles grow over hidden mine fields there exists a curious freedom. Between the guns of the deployed powers, between the march of patrols and policing dogs there is an uncultivated strip of land from which law and man himself have retreated. Along this uneasy border the old life of the wild has come back into its own. Weeds grow and animals slip about in the night where no man dares to hunt them. A thin uncertain line fringes the edge of oppression. The freedom it contains is fit only for birds and floating thistledown or a wandering fox. Nevertheless there must be men who look upon it with envy.

The imagination can grasp this faint underscoring of freedom but there are few who realize that precisely similar lines run in a delicate tracery along every civilized road in the West, or that these hedges of thorn apple and osage orange are the last refuge of wild life between the cultivated fields of civilization. It takes a refugee at heart, a

3

wistful glancer over fences, to sense this one dimensional world, but it is there. I can attest to it for I myself am such a fugitive.

This confession need alarm no one. I am relatively harmless. I have not broken or entered, or passed illegally over boundaries. I am not on the lists of the police. The only time that I have gazed into the wrong end of a gun I have been the injured party. Even this episode, however, took place many years ago and was in another country at the hands of foreigners. In spite of this, I repeat that I am a fugitive. I was born one.

The world will say that this is impossible, that fugitives are made by laws and acts of violence, that without these preliminaries no man can be called a fugitive, that without pursuit no man can be hunted. It may be so. Nevertheless I know that there are men born to hunt and some few born to flee, whether physically or mentally makes no difference. That is purely a legal quibble. The fact that I wear the protective coloration of sedate citizenship is a ruse of the fox—I learned it long ago. The facts of my inner life are quite otherwise. Early, very early, the consciousness of this difference emerges. This is how it began for me.

It begins in the echoing loneliness of a house with no other children; in the silence of a deafened mother; in the child head growing strangely aware of itself as it prattled over immense and solitary games. The child learned that there were shadows in the closets and a green darkness behind the close-drawn curtains of the parlor; he was aware of a cool twilight in the basement. He was afraid only of noise.

Noise is the Outside—the bully in the next block by whose house you had to pass in order to go to school. Noise is all the things you did not wish to do. It is the games in which you were pummeled by other children's big brothers, it is the sharp, demanding voices of adults who snatch your books. Noise is day. And out of that intolerable sunlight your one purpose has been given—to escape. Few men have such motivations in childhood, few are so constantly seeking for the loophole in the fern where the leaves swing shut behind them. But I anticipate. It is in the mind that the flight commences. It is there that the arc lights lay their shadows. It is there, down those streets past unlit houses that the child runs on alone.

II

We stood in a wide flat field at sunset. For the life of me I can remember no other children before them. I must have run away and been playing by myself until I had wandered to the edge of the town. They were older than I and knew where they came from and how to get back. I joined them.

They were not going home. They were going to a place called Green Gulch. They came from some other part of town, and their clothes were rough, their eyes worldly and sly. I think, looking back, that it must have been a little like a child following goblins home to their hill at nightfall, but nobody threatened me. Besides, I was very small and did not know the way home, so I followed them.

Presently we came to some rocks. The place was well named. It was a huge pool in a sandstone basin, green and dark with the evening over it and the trees leaning secretly inward above the water. When you looked down, you saw the sky. I remember that place as it was when we came there. I remember the quiet and the green ferns touching the green water. I remember we played there, innocently at first.

But someone found the spirit of the place, a huge old turtle, asleep in the ferns. He was the last lord of the green water before the town poured over it. I saw his end.

They pounded him to death with stones on the other side of the pool while I looked on in stupefied horror. I had never seen death before.

Suddenly, as I stood there small and uncertain and frightened, a grimy, splattered gnome who had been stooping over the turtle stood up with a rock in his hand. He looked at me, and around that little group some curious evil impulse passed like a wave. I felt it and drew back. I was alone there. They were not human.

I do not know who threw the first stone, who splashed water over my suit, who struck me first, or even who finally, among that ring of vicious faces, put me on my feet, dragged me to the roadside, pointed and said, roughly, "There's your road, kid, follow the street lamps. They'll take you home."

They stood in a little group watching me, nervous now, ashamed a little at the ferocious pack impulse toward the outsider that had swept over them.

I never forgot that moment.

I went because I had to, down that road with the wind moving in the fields. I went slowly from one spot of light to another and in between I thought the things a child thinks, so that I did not stop at any house nor ask anyone to help me when I came to the lighted streets.

I had discovered evil. It was a monstrous and corroding knowledge. It could not be told to adults because it was the evil of childhood in which no one believes. I was alone with it in the dark. And in the dark henceforth, in some fashion, I was destined to stay until, two years later, I found the gold wheel. I played alone in those days, particularly after my rejection by the boys who regarded Green Gulch as their territory. I took to creeping up alleys and peering through hedges. I was not miserable. There was a wonderful compensating secrecy about these activities. I had little shelters in hedgerows and I knew and perfected secret entrances and exits into the most amazing worlds.

There was, for example, the Rudd mansion. I never saw the inside of it, but I made the discovery that in a stone incinerator, back of the house and close up to the immense hedge through which I had worked a passage, there were often burned toys. Apparently the Rudd family lived with great prodigality and cast recklessly away what to me were invaluable possessions. I got in the habit of creeping through the hedge at nightfall and scratching in the ashes for bits of Meccano sets and other little treasures which I would bear homeward.

One frosty night in early fall I turned up a gold wheel. It was not gold really, but I pretended it was. To me it represented all those things—perhaps in a dim way life itself—that are denied by poverty. The wheel had been part of a child's construction set of some sort. It was grooved to run on a track and it had a screw on the hub to enable it to be fitted adjustably to an axle. The amalgam of which it was made was hard and golden and it had come untouched through the incinerator fires. In my childish world it was a wonderful object and I haunted the incinerator for many nights thereafter hoping I might secure the remaining wheel. The flow of toys declined, however, and I never found the second gold wheel. The one I had found became a sort of fetish which I carried around with me. I had become very conscious of gold wheels and finally I made up my mind to run away upon a pair of them.

My decision came about through the appearance in our neighborhood of a tea wagon which used to stop once or twice a week at the house next door. This was not an ordinary delivery wagon. It was a neatly enclosed cart and at the rear beneath a latched door was a little step for the convenience of the driver when he wished to come around in back and secure the packages of tea which he sold.

Two things occupied my attention at once. First, the little footboard was of just the right height and size to permit a small boy to sit upon it and ride away unseen once

the driver had taken the reins and seated himself at the
front of the cart. In addition, the wheels of the cart were
large and long-spoked and painted a bright golden yellow.
When the horse broke into a spanking trot those wheels
spun and glittered in the equally golden air of autumn
with an irresistible attraction. Upon that rear step I had
made my decision to launch out into the world. It was not
the product of a momentary whim. I studied for several
days the habits of the tea man until I knew the moment to
run forward and perch upon the step. It never crossed my
mind to concern myself with where he was going. Such
adult matters happily never troubled me. It was enough to
be gone between a pair of spinning golden wheels.

On the appointed day, without provision for the future
and with a renewed sublime trust in the permanence of
sunshine and all good and golden things, I essayed my first
great venture into the outer wilderness. My mother was
busy with her dishes in the kitchen. As the tea wagon
drew up to the house next door I loitered by a bush in the
front yard. When the driver leapt once more upon his box
I swung hastily upon the little step at the rear. There was
no flaw in my escape. The horse trotted with increasing
speed over the cobbles, the wheels spun on either side of
me in the sunshine, and I was off through the city traffic,
followed by the amused or concerned stares of adults
along the street. I jounced and bumped but my hold was
secure. Horseshoes rang and the whole bright world was
one glitter of revolving gold. I had never clearly dealt with
the problem of what I would do if the driver continued to
make stops, but now it appeared such fears were ground-
less. There were no more stops. The wheels spun faster
and faster. We were headed for the open countryside.

It was, I think, the most marvelous ride I shall ever
make in this life. I can still hear the pounding echo of the
horse's hoofs over wooden bridges. Shafts of light—it was
growing cloudy now—moved over the green meadows by

the roadside. I have traversed that road many times since, but the green is faded, the flowers ordinary. On that day, however, we were moving through the kind of eternal light which exists only in the minds of the very young. I remember one other queer thing about that journey: the driver made no impression on my mind at all. I do not recall a cry, a crack of the whip, anything to indicate his genuine presence. We went clopping steadily down a long hill, and up, up against the sky where black clouds were beginning to boil and billow with the threat of an oncoming storm. Far up on that great hill I had a momentary flash of memory. We were headed for the bishop's house.

The bishop's house, which lay thus well out into the country beside an orphanage, was a huge place of massive stone so well set and timeless that it gave the appearance of having been there before the city was built. I had heard my elders speak of it with a touch of awe in their voices. It had high battlements of red granite and around the yard ran a black iron fence through which, according to story, only the baptized might pass. Inside, accepted by my childish mind, was another somewhat supernatural world shut off by hedges.

As we wound higher along the skyline I could see the ruts in the road wriggle, diverge, and merge beneath my dangling feet. Because of my position at the rear of the cart it was impossible to see ahead. The first drops of rain were beginning to make little puffs of dirt in the road and finally as we slowed to a walk on the drive leading up to the gates the storm caught up to us in a great gust of wind and driving rain.

With scarce a pause the iron gates swung open for the tea wagon. I heard the horseshoes ringing on the stones of the drive as I leaped from my perch on the little step and darted into the safety of the hedge. The thunder from the clouds mingled with the hollow rolling of the wheels and the crash of the closing gates before me echoed through my frightened head with a kind of dreadful finality. It was only then, in the intermittent flashes of the lightning, that I realized I was not alone.

In the hedge where I crouched beside the bishop's gate were many hundreds of brown birds, strangers, sitting immovable and still. They paid no attention to me. In fact, they were immersed in a kind of waiting silence so secret and immense that I was much too overawed to disturb them. Instead, I huddled into this thin world beneath the birds while the storm leaped and flickered as though hesitating whether to harry us out of our refuge into the rolling domain of the clouds. Today I know that those birds were migrating and had sought shelter from exhaustion. On that desolate countryside they had come unerringly down upon the thin line of the bishop's hedge.

The tea wagon had unaccountably vanished. The storm after a time grumbled its way slowly into the distance and with equal slowness I crept unwillingly out into the wet road and began my long walk homeward. I felt in the process some obscure sense of loss. It was as though I had been on the verge of a great adventure into another world that had eluded me; the green light had passed away from the fields. I thought once wistfully of the gold wheel I had failed to find and that seemed vaguely linked to my predicament. I was destined to see it only once in the years that followed—those mature years in which, slower and slower, dimmer and dimmer, the fancies and passions of childhood fade away into the past. Strangely enough, it returned in a moment of violence.

III

The event was simple. There were three of us, jammed into the seat of a stripped car. We were doing fifty miles an hour over a stretch of open grassland, while ahead of us still flashed the white hindquarters of a running antelope. There was no road; no signs, no warnings. There was only the green fenceless unrolling plain and that elusive steel-hearted beast dancing away before us.

The driver pushed the pedal toward the floor.

"You can kill him from here," he said and gestured toward the rifle on my lap.

I did not want to kill him. I looked for a barrier, a fence, an obstacle to wheels, something to stop this game while it was still fun. I wanted to see that unscathed animal go over a hedge and vanish, leaving maybe a little wisp of fur on a thorn to let us know he had passed unharmed out of our reach.

I shrugged and said carefully, indifferently, for I knew the man I rode with, "Why hurry? We'll get him all right in the end."

The driver grunted and started to shift his weight once more upon the pedal. It was just then, in one final brake-screaming instant, that I saw the barrier. It was there and our beast had already cleared it without changing his stride. It was the barrier between life and death.

There was a gulch five feet wide and maybe eight feet deep coming up to meet us, its edge well hidden in the prairie grass. As we saw it we struck, the front wheels colliding and exploding against the opposite bank. By some freak of pressures we remained there stunned, the bumper holding us above the pit. In that moment, as my head snapped nearly into blackness, I saw a loose golden wheel rolling and rolling on the prairie grass. In my ears there resounded the thunder of the tea wagon pounding over the cobbles and the clang of the bishop's iron gate in the midst of the storm. Then the rumbling receded into the distance and I wiped the blood from my nose.

"He's gone," someone said stupidly.

I put my hands against the bent dashboard and shook my head to clear it.

"The man with the tea wagon?" I asked before I thought.

"The buck," someone answered a long way off, his voice a little thickened. "That buck stepped across the ravine like it wasn't there. We damn near stopped for good. It's like an invisible wall, a line you can't see."

"Yes," I said.

But I didn't say I had wished for it. I didn't say that I remembered how the birds sit on those lines and you never knew which side the birds were on because they sat so quietly and were waiting. You had to be a fugitive to know this and to know the lines were everywhere—a net running through one's brain as well as the outside world. Someday I would pass through the leaves into the open when I should have stayed under the hedge with the birds.

With an effort I lifted the rifle and climbed stiffly out, looking all around the horizon like a hunter. I wear, you see, the protective coloring of men. It is a ruse of the fox —I learned it long ago.

2

THE PLACES BELOW

I

IF you cannot bear the silence and the darkness, do not go there; if you dislike black night and yawning chasms, never make them your profession. If you fear the sound of water hurrying through crevices toward unknown and mysterious destinations, do not consider it. Seek out the sunshine. It is a simple prescription. Avoid the darkness.

It is a simple prescription, but you will not follow it. You will turn immediately to the darkness. You will be drawn to it by cords of fear and of longing. You will imagine that you are tired of the sunlight; the waters that unnerve you will tug in the ancient recesses of your mind; the midnight will seem restful—you will end by going down.

15

I am a case of this sort. Choices, more choices than we like afterward to believe, are made far backward in the innocence of childhood. It has been so with me, as, doubtless, it has been so with you. There was a Washington eccentric in the 1920s whose underground tunnels caused a great stir in the newspapers when someone stumbled upon them. He constructed them himself in his spare time. At first the reporters and police thought they were the work of spies. Afterward it developed that the secret passages were the harmless hobby of an elderly professor. They led nowhere.

I should like to have met that man. He was one of us. To have set out alone with a shovel shows the depth of his need. But there are easier ways into the earth, and passages that run farther. Let me tell you of one of them.

II

The house lies on the edge of a rolling plain. It is an old, warm farmhouse where people rock on the porch in the starry evenings. There is no shadow on it; it is lived in, complete, normal. But it has a cellar, and that cellar has a monster in it. Or something that gives you the same feeling as a monster. I have been there many times. I know men who would not live in a house with a cellar like that. The owner and I understand each other. He knows why I come. If it has been a long time, I question him with my eyes. He nods or he shakes his head, depending upon the conditions below.

"It is better now," he ventures as we go around to the back of the house. "If it drops any lower we may be able to get into the Blue Room."

We never actually get there, of course, but we talk that way. Only once in the course of many years did I find him awed by what he had seen. He came down the front steps that time and hurried to meet me. "It came up the cellar stairs last night, Doctor. In the night. A hundred feet in three hours. You can't go down. Not this season."

But mostly it is not like that. The cellar seems ordinary at first glance—a little deeper than some. Then you take another turn at the stairs and the air seems to grow damp. There is a faint sulphur smell, and the steps, you begin to perceive, are cut out of living rock.

There is a mark on them now. The mark where what was below came up the cellar stairs one night. You listen again to his story and feel the creep of some uneasy power in the rocks below. Then you go down.

You go down zigzagging and sliding through some accidental tremendous fissure torn in the bowels of the earth. Great stones teeter over you. This is the country of Charon and Cerberus; from this the pleasant fields draw sustenance. A country wit has scrawled a pointing arrow on a rock: "Ten miles to hell." Oddly, you do not laugh. The sulphur smell grows stronger. There, suddenly, your journey ends.

A great pool of cold blue water lies before you. It is so clear that if you were not warned you would march into it, following the splendor of that vast, blue chamber that glistens and invites you from below. You stand on the edge of a country you will never enter in the flesh. Its pale blue galleries seem to speak faintly of faces you will never see. It invites you as arsenical springs invite the thirsty. Nostalgia fills your soul. You reach a hand into the water. The distances are greater than they seem.

"It always stays about here," your guide explains plaintively, pointing at the water's edge. "Once it went down about ten feet and I thought sure we were going to get in. But it came back. It always does. I been watchin' my whole life an' I'm never going to see it all. Nobody's ever going to get in there—not to the Blue Room.

"And when it came up that time afterward it was almost like it was going to show us. My God, that cold blue came right up the tunnel, over the lights and almost out of the house. You could see the lights glowing way back there in a hundred feet of water, before they went out. I thought the damn thing was comin' out the front door, wasn't ever goin' to stop, but it did. It stopped there on that landing like something fumbling for a key. Then by and by it turned and went back. A little at a time, but slow, slow enough to show us. It was a year before we saw the Blue Room."

The Blue Room. It was his single obsession, as it was that of anyone who came there too often. A corner of his brain was eerie with stalactites and that wavering world of distance and promises. He knows me well now when I come up the steps. We are both older. We will never see that chamber as it really is. There is nothing like it in the fields or in the sunlight. It is a part of the places below. And whether the places below lie in the dark of an old cellar or in the crypts and recesses of the mind, or whether they are a glimmering reflection of both together, he does not know any longer. When we have reached the state of mind of that elderly professor with his shovel, sometime, perhaps, we will wade slowly down and see. . . .

There are blind fish that have chosen this world and prefer to live there. There are crickets as white as the fungi under rotting boards. There are bats that turn their little goblin faces uneasily in the glow of your lamp and squeak down at you protestingly. There is the world of light and the world of darkness. And some in the world of light prefer the darkness. That is why the old man shoveled his way downward beneath a staid Washington mansion; that is why men come and stare at the Blue Room. I have said that the choice begins in the innocence of childhood. This is how it began for me.

III

The brain is a strange instrument. The things it chooses to remember are as fantastic as the things it chooses to forget. I have not been in that city for over a score of years. I have not been below, in the dripping labyrinth that underlies its streets, since I was ten. Yet lying on my bed at midnight, waiting for sleep, I find myself retracing in memory each twist and turn of the storm drains underneath the sunlit streets that other men remember. I know how sounds can amplify in that darkness and become terrible. My skin creeps from the water and the mud.

My memory is a rat's memory scurrying with disembodied alacrity through a hollow maze of tubes that exist now only in my head. It turns right and left unerringly. It knows the one way out of a chamber where four black openings yawn simultaneously. Sometimes in that chamber a candle flickers, lighting momentarily another sweat-streaked desperate face.

I never see the face completely, though once I knew it well. Perhaps it is the reluctance of remembered terror. Perhaps it is because the face itself is gone. Nevertheless if I strain consciously to remember, I can remember. It is the face of the Rat. It is true I could run the corridors and follow candle glimmerings. But the Rat was my lord and master. He created a world—the world I live in—and he died and left me in it.

He spoke to me on the day we moved into that neighborhood. He was deceptively slight of build, with the terrible intensity of a coiled spring. His face, even, had the quivering eagerness of some small, quick animal.

"You can join our gang," he said.

I was shy with the shyness of many rebuffs. "Thanks," I said. And then, warily, "I don't play ball very good. D'ya 'spose they'll let me?"

"C'mon," he said.

We went down through a waste of weeds in a back lot. There were big red granite boulders from an old house lying there. A couple of kids were pecking pictures and signs on them with a stone.

"Why don't you use a knife or a chisel?" I asked, trying to be helpful.

"Can't," said the Rat scornfully.

"Why not?" I protested.

"We're cavemen. Those are cave pictures. See? 'Stinct animals. You can't use a chisel. Cavemen didn't have no chisels. We're gonna be just like 'em. No chisels either."

He eyed me challengingly. "You wanta be a caveman?"

"Why sure," I said, "only I don't know how. Where are the caves? What do we do?" I belonged to something at last. I was a caveman.

"C'mon," they said. "And don't ever tell your mother."

"Okay," I said. That was easy.

"Cross your heart?"

"Okay," I said. And that one was for always, though I didn't know it.

"I'm the Rat," said the Rat, dispassionately. "This is my gang and you're in it. But 'fore you get a name you gotta prove your guts. You gotta go down under the ground. You ain't afraid of the dark, are ya?"

The group measured me. I eyed them back uneasily. "No," I said. "What do you mean undertheground?"

"Undertheground's real, you'll see all right," said the Rat.

"C'mon," they clamored, moving off through the weeds. My heart knocked a little. "I'm coming," I said.

That did it, you see. It wasn't too late then. I could have gone home, and I wouldn't have these dreams now or go down to look at the Blue Room. But I ran along after them through the weeds, shouting. It takes just that, in some unwary instant, to telescope fifty thousand years. Afterward you wonder how to get back. I doubt if the Rat ever managed it for himself. Not after seeing the way he went into that pipe.

It was the vent to twenty square miles of sky when the rains blew up. It emptied at the edge of a lake, and it ran two miles back under the town before the labyrinth began. It was dark as a vanished geological era, and in a heavy rain the pipes filled and thundered like Niagara. You didn't stay in the sewers then—not if you wanted to live— and you took good care not to get caught where you couldn't scramble out a few minutes after a storm hit.

That was the world we lived in. We never told Mother, and we avoided Father. We scrounged our own candles; we dragged food into these abysses. We scratched tribal symbols on the big tiles by candlelight, as the Rat directed. We raided other bands and retreated through the sewer network. We lived as men may sometime live in the ruins of New York.

I learned from the Rat what it was about. It seemed that a long time ago everybody had lived this way. Why they had quit was a mystery to me. The Rat couldn't answer that one. His reading hadn't progressed that far.

IV

It dawned a clear day on the morning the world ended. I suppose it must have happened that way when the Neanderthals left their caves for the last time, with the big ice moving down. I figure they expected to come back, but something happened. It was like that with the Rat and myself.

We were down there after breakfast exploring through a side tunnel a quarter filled with sand and standing water. It was bad going in a place we wouldn't have been in without a glance at the sky before coming down. But the sky had been cloudless. The Rat was a good leader that way, foresighted and sharp. I'd guess we were six hundred feet into this tunnel, laboring along on hands and knees and sometimes writhing our way over a sand bar when the Rat, who was ahead of me with the candle, held it up and said, "Listen." We stopped dead. I could see the straining intensity flicker on the Rat's thin face as he turned the candle toward me.

The tunnel dripped a little and at first I heard nothing. The Rat jabbed at me. "Listen, for Christ's sake," he said. I heard it then all right, and my heart gave a big jump and almost stopped altogether, but it was a very little sound. It was nothing but a little murmuring in the water, a little whisper, a little complaint as though the water were growing restless and wanted to go somewhere.

"It's moving," I said, and the Rat said nothing at all except to cast the light forward as far as he could. The darkness swallowed it up and the murmuring sounded louder, except maybe it was the blood in our ears.

We listened again and there seemed to be a far-off pouring noise muffled by sand and distance. We were only ten years old, and suddenly this place was very narrow and we were tired of playing like men. I might have cried, but the Rat just poked me and said "C'mon" as he always did. I scrambled at his heels and somehow we kept the candle burning looking for something bigger to get into. This was a low pipe. It wouldn't take much to fill it, and you couldn't move very fast. Just try to crawl a couple of blocks on your stomach sometime and you'll see what I mean.

The water kept on moving with us and talking to us in that slightly, just slightly, sinister way it had. This was just the starter. Where had that instantaneous storm come from, and what was blowing it up? There was no use asking down there. The water would tell us soon enough. It did. It began to rise a little. One could hear a pouring thunder in the outer drain.

We were just a couple of leaping automatons now, going forward in the only way we could go—with the pipe. Our clothes were shredded by the little needles in the tile. Our knees were raw flesh, our hands were bruised. We whimpered to ourselves through the talking water, but there was little breath to whimper with. We were almost spent, and the minute we were spent we would go under. It was, by actual measurement, a hundred and fifty feet to where we reached the chamber. Speeding as we were, it could hardly have taken us five minutes. By heart and lungs and brain it was an hour.

The Rat got there first and reached and dragged me. We staggered upright in the water. The water was low and spread out over the chamber floor. It only lapped our ankles. Time was still with us, but what should we do? The candle sputtered and showed us three openings the size of the one out of which we had lunged. We could go into one of them and still be trapped and drowned.

Overhead in the darkness was a street manhole. Was it locked shut, and if not, could we lift it? If we didn't and this was a big rain, the chamber would fill. I knew it would. I had peered many times into such maelstroms. It would not only fill, the suction would be irresistible. We would be swept back into the underground.

Staggering, I got the Rat on my shoulders. He heaved against the cover lid. It stirred a little, but nothing happened. The Rat slid panting down into my arms.

We leaned against the pipes a moment, too exhausted to speak. The stream continued to pour past our ankles.

Finally in one despairing burst of energy we each climbed on the protruding edge of a pipe and pushed against the manhole cover. Reluctantly it gave. We shoved it aside and sprawled gasping into the street.

Spent as we were, we leaped from the pavement in amazement. The hot tar burned. The sky was clear. The gutters in the street were dry. Astounded, we looked farther along the street. A city employee had opened a fire hydrant for testing. The water was spouting from a plug into a nearby drain.

A voice interrupted us. It was the voice of my father. "Son," he said with suppressed fury, "I've told you before to keep out of sewers. Look at you. Look at both of you. You're coming home. By god I'm telling you you're *staying* home."

"Yes, Father," I said. I took his hand as he marched me along. *If you fear the sound of water hurrying toward unknown and mysterious destinations do not go there.* "Undisciplined, completely undisciplined," my father muttered, still unmollified. "Yes, Father," I said, clutching him more tightly. I liked the strength in his hand.

V

It is a simple prescription, but you will not follow it. The urge returns. The same voices speak to you. It was true we had left the sewers. Our parents had seen to that. Besides, we were growing too big to navigate them successfully. Down by an old orphanage, however, I found a new opening. It was a drain all right, and it was old. It was not part of the system we knew. It was brick and big enough to stand upright in. There was green moss around the entrance and on the bricks inside. I went in just a few steps and saw that it was dark and that it ran off under the hill. Then I went and got the Rat.

It was like a green door and the air blew out of it cold and smelling of water on a hot midsummer day. We dropped into the brush that covered the opening from sight and listened, looking at each other. Then we went in on tiptoe, the Rat leading as always. We went over the moss like velvet and that air kept blowing cool and clean.

We lost sight of the entrance. It just faded out in a kind of green twilight. We must have been a hundred yards in when the Rat stopped. I knew what he wanted, and we listened. From somewhere up ahead I could hear it—the vibration of falling water—and the air now with a little chill.

I didn't want to see it, where that water was going, I mean, or why it was in this hill. I had had enough of the green door. But I would follow the Rat anywhere. So I waited, standing on one foot and then the other.

"We can come back later with the gang," I ventured. The Rat turned and looked at me and through me and beyond me. He tapped my arm, and I could see the thin, quizzical line deepen on his sharp forehead. "We'll keep it for our own," he said. "Just us." Then he turned, and we left that sound vibrating in the air and went back to the world.

A few weeks later he was dead—dead of some casual childhood illness. All that consuming energy and passionate intellectual hunger had come to nothing. In later years places of learning would become familiar sights to me. I never met a mind like his again.

Once after his death I went to the green door. It was still secret and that cool draft came up from below. I stood a moment on the moss at the entrance. "Just us," the Rat had said, and it warmed me a little. But it was no use without the Rat. I backed out and turned away.

Something had swung behind me then, but I didn't know it. You find those things out by degrees in the passage to manhood, in the way you continue to pick up

stones or linger at dark openings. If there is any truth to
the story that at death men return to the period they have
loved best in life, I know well where I will awake. It will
be somewhere on the cold, bleak uplands of the ice-age
world, by the fire in the cave, and the watching eyes without. It was the Rat who left me there.

I knew it finally in the Hall of Shadows, in a cave I had
no business to be in. By what road I had crept there I had
scant knowledge. By what way I would get out I was not
sure. Yet something drew me—it was drawing me more
and more. My work did not demand that I take that turning under the ledge or chance that passage downward. I
was an archaeologist—not a fool.

Yet there I lay on my back, finally, and the outside
world seemed far away and infinitely wearying as a place to
which to return. I was in a room meant for a king's burial.
I lay on the floor of an enormous chamber, but a chamber
across which one could not move except by crawling. For
that great hall was hung with vast tapestries and heavy
curtains over which my lantern played. And those tapestries were iridescent stone. The powers that had built that
chamber in the depths of the mountain were closing it
again. I had come as the curtains lingered above the floor.
If I stayed they would descend.

Some in the world of light desire the darkness. I saw
that then more clearly than before. The whole infinite ladder of life was filled with this backward yearning. There
were the mammals who had given up the land and returned to the sea; there were fish that slept in the mud,
birds that no longer flew. Probably also there had been
hairy men who wept when fashion tore them from their
caverns. I loved the darkness. I feared it, yet returned to
it. It was the mother out of which I came. From
somewhere under those moveless curtains, in that utter
darkness beneath the stone, a small breeze blew. It was

cool, and there was a faint sound of water in it—far off, menacing, and sweet. It invited me forward. It urged me to crawl on. For the first time in years I remembered the green door and the Rat as he stood there listening. The Rat who had eyed me shrewdly, saying "just us." What had he heard there in the falling water? And what had he meant?

The same door was before me now—that door through which the Rat had gone. I waited as I had waited long ago at that other entrance, but this time, as before, no one came over the green moss like velvet; no one touched my arm. I waited, but there was no one to help me. One entered by oneself, or not at all.

The air blew cool on my sweating forehead, and that far-off murmur that might have come through remote distances of stone still urged me onward, but I think it whispered in my brain and not the Hall. Slowly, with agonizing reluctance, I drew backward. Slowly I began to crawl toward daylight, along the way I had come.

3

BIG EYES
AND SMALL EYES

"THIS is your house," says the poet Conrad Aiken, and you know he is talking about the human skull. "On one side there is darkness," he warns you; "on one side there is light." He wrote better than he knew, that sad-voiced man, for nature had pondered the problem before him. On the table as I write lies the skull of a relative of ours, a spectral creature which flits from tree to tree in the night-time forests of Borneo. It is about the size of a kitten's skull, but it possesses a most remarkable feature. If the human cranium were built to similar proportions, every aspect of the human face would be squeezed to provide for two great bony saucers with projecting rims. These saucers would occupy and extend far beyond the area now represented by our eye sockets. We would then possess the enormous owl eyes of a creature who is totally nocturnal but who must leap and spring about in the midnight darkness of a tropical rain forest.

This is your house, said nature, in essence, to the spectral tarsier, and the light, what there is of it, must be made to come in. This is your house, she also said to man, but your eyes will be day eyes. You will not need to cherish every beam of moonlight, or the spark of a star through a leaf. You will see what you must, but leave the dark alone. So this far-off relative of ours, with the thin and delicate fingers of a man, lives the life of a ghost. And man, who bumps his head and fumbles in the dark because of his small day-born eyes, fears the ghosts of the dark above all things. As a consequence, my confession is that of a man with night fear, and it is also the confession of a very large proportion of the human race.

In a way it is the fear of the tide, the night tide, I call it, because that is the way you come to feel it—invisible, imperceptible almost, unless it is looked for—and yet, as you grow older you realize that it is always there, swirling like vapor just beyond the edge of the lamp at evening and similarly out to the ends of the universe. Or at least it gives you that kind of sensation—a need to huddle in somewhere with a light.

Maybe that is the real reason why men string lamps far out into country lanes and try to run down everything with red eyes that happens to waddle across the road in front of their headlights. It is cruel but revelatory: we are insecure, and this is our warfare with the dark. It began when man first lit a fire at a cave mouth and the eyes he feared—very big eyes they were then—began to blink and draw back. So he lights and lights in a passion for illumination that is insatiable—a poor day-born thing contending against one of the greatest powers in the universe. Even man's own domestic animals, the creatures he has chosen to bring in to the fire beside him, grow suspect in the evening. His cat hunts alone through the weeds, and his dog whines and snuffles at the door. They all have that allegiance to the dark. They are never wholly his.

When you really get the swell of the night tide, however, is at the moment it comes right in upon you and swirls, figuratively at least, around your ankles. Rats play a good part in such episodes, because they are the real agents of the night and there is a sort of malign intelligence about them that is frightening. Also, they have a particularly bold way of paying visits to men after nightfall, as though they wanted to remind us of something waiting and not very pleasant.

Many years ago a friend of mine took a room in an obscure hotel in the heart of a great city. There was a blaze of street lights outside, and a few shadows. He had opened the window and retired, he told me, when something soft and heavy dropped on his feet as he lay stretched out in bed. Though he admittedly was startled, it occurred to him that the creature on his legs might be a friendly tomcat from the fire escape. He tried to estimate the weight of the crouched body from under his blankets and resisted a frightened impulse to spring up. He spoke soothingly into the dark, for he liked cats, and reached for a match at his bedside table.

The match flared, and in that moment a sewer rat as big as a house cat sat up on its haunches and glared into the match flame with pink demoniac eyes. That one match flare, so my friend told me afterward, seemed to last the lifetime of the human race. Then the match went out and he simultaneously hurtled from the bed. From his incoherent account of what happened afterward I suspect that both rat and man left by the window but fortunately, perhaps, not at the same instant. That sort of thing, you know, is like getting a personal message from the dark. You are apt to remember it a lifetime.

Or, speaking of rats, take what happened to me. It is true I was not confronted by this rat eye to eye in a match flame, but on the other hand there was an even more frightening *intellectual* quality about the situation. And again the creature arrived, like a messenger from space, at an appropriate point in a very significant conversation. He addressed himself to me for the very simple reason that I was the only one in a position to see him. I will call him Conlin's rat, in order to protect the good name of a distinguished American novelist who was unaware of the low company he kept.

This man is capable of most eloquent discourse. The evening was perfect. The light was just fading on the faces of the company, and the perfectly clipped lawns and hedges fell away before us on the terrace as only the very rich and the very powerful can afford to have them. My friend held a mint julep in his hand and gestured toward me.

"Man," he said, "will turn the whole earth into a garden for his own enjoyment. It is just a question of time. I admit the obstacles you have mentioned, but I have tremendous faith in man. He will win through. I drink to him."

He poised his glass and said other happy and felicitous things to which the company present raised their glasses. Even my own glass—and I am a weak and doubting character—was somewhat dubiously being lifted, when I saw an incredible and revolting sight. There, under my friend's white canvas chair, and outlined against the stuccoed wall at his back, a thin, greasy, wet-backed rat upreared himself and twitched his whiskers with a cynical contempt for all that white-gowned, well-clothed company.

I say he addressed himself to me, for I have never seen anything so peculiarly appropriate. He had obviously emerged from a drain a bit farther on in the wall, perhaps a little prematurely, along with the rising tide of evening. I stared in unbelief and waited for the ladies to scream. I wanted to lift my glass. I wanted to set it down. I waited for my novelist friend to come to his senses and spring away from that bewhiskered mocking animal that crouched beneath him. The novelist made no move. He spoke on as eloquently as always, while the rat sniffed his shoe and listened, stretching up to his full height. I felt for an uneasy moment that the creature might ironically applaud. He looked across at me, and it seemed best not to warn the company. Anyway, it was unlikely that I could warn them sufficiently.

For that this was a message I felt certain. I alone saw him and I never spoke. He listened a while with great attentiveness to our voices, and then he went back into the rising darkness and the drain pipe swallowed him up. But you can see what I mean by a tide and how with the dark it comes in around your ankles. Light the lights, I always say, but I have found that even this is no real security—not in the night. Because in the end you may find that the remaining light has only allowed you to see something it would have been better not to see at all.

Take, for instance, the time that I saw the black beetle. I repeat that "light the lights" is my motto, so when this fit of insomnia came on me I retired to the living room, my wife not sharing my view of the universe at three in the morning, and settled down to read T. K. Oesterreich's *Demoniacal Possession*.

This was assuredly not bravado on my part. It was just that as a professor I had to give a lecture on primitive religion in the morning, and this seemed as good a time as any to "get on with it," as my dean is always saying. I snapped my small reading lamp to the lowest power and crept into what I thought in my innocence was its charmed and healthy circle of light.

I had been reading for about an hour and was pretty well into the business of familiars, recognizable signs of demonic intrusion, shape-shifting and other supernatural phenomena, when I saw something moving along the edge of my vision. Now to understand this episode you have to realize where it took place. We then lived high up in an apartment house that is noted for its cleanliness; I had never seen a mouse or a roach in the kitchen, let alone in the living room.

I did not believe, therefore, in what began to march across my circle of green light as though conjuring itself into existence. In fact, I pulled my feet up in the chair and leaned down until I was practically standing on my head. It was no illusion. A huge black bug—not a roach, but a fat-bodied and particularly odious beetle of dubious affinities—was marching right across the carpet under my nose. Before I could adjust my bifocals and marshal the necessary militancy which my wife is generally on hand to supply, the creature waddled with the most absolute surety under the heavy green chest in the living room and disappeared.

I have never seen the beetle since, and my wife, who forced me to move the chest, absolutely denies his existence. I know better, but I am willing to admit now that people may have a point who refuse to turn on lights in the dark. At three in the morning, my wife says, what do you expect to see if you turn on a light? My only retort to this is the rather obvious one that she will have to think what may be there if she does not turn on the light.

This does not affect my wife in the least, but it does me. I get to thinking about it and feel impelled to snap on a switch and look, just in case . . . My wife, however, is a genuinely daylight person. She has never had the slightest interest in this dark world over the border except to pursue all its manifestations, like the black beetle, with an exterminating broom. My own viewpoint, I like to think, is rather more traveled. I have been over into that nocturnal country, as I will presently recount, and though I stand in awe of it, it has also stimulated my curiosity. In fact, though I hesitate to speak openly of the matter, I have a faint, though not too secure, feeling of kinship with certain creatures I have encountered there.

Sometimes in a country lane at midnight you can sense their eyes upon you—the eyes that by daylight may be the vacuous protuberant orbs of grazing cattle or the good brown eyes of farm dogs. But there, in the midnight lane, they draw off from you or silently watch you pass from their hidden coverts in the hedgerows. They are back in a secret world from which man has been shut out, and they want no truck with him after nightfall. Perhaps it is because of this that more and more we employ machines with lights and great noise to rush by these watchful shadows. My experience, therefore, may be among the last to be reported from that night world, which, with our machines to face, is slowly ebbing back into little patches of wilderness behind lighted signboards. It concerns a journey. I will not say where the journey began, but it took place in the years that have come to be called the Great Depression and was made alone and on foot. Finally I had come to a place where, far off over an endless blue plain, I could see the snow on the crests of the mountains. The city to which I was journeying lay, I knew, at the foot of the highest peak. I would keep the mountains in sight, I thought to myself, and find my own path to the city.

I climbed over a barbed-wire fence and marched directly toward the city through the blue air under the great white peak. I think sometimes now, long afterward, that it was the happiest, most independent day of my entire life. No one waited for me anywhere. I was complete in myself like a young migrating animal whose world exists totally in the present moment. The range with its drifting cattle and an occasional passing bird began to unroll beneath my stride. I meant to be across that range and over an escarpment of stone to the city at the mountain's foot before the dawn of another morning. During the entire walk I was never to meet another human being. The lights and showers of that high landscape, the moving shadows of clouds, shone upon or darkened my face alternately, but I was destined to share the experience with no one.

In the later afternoon, after descending into innumerable arroyos and scrambling with difficulty up the vertical bank of the opposite side, I began to grow tired. Coming out finally into a country that was less trenched and eroded, I was trudging steadily onward when I came upon a pond. At least for all purposes it could answer to the name, though it was only a few inches deep—mere standing rainwater caught in a depression of impermeable soil and interspersed with tufts of brown buffalo grass. I hesitated by it for a moment, somewhat disturbed by a few leeches which I could see moving among the grass stems. Then, losing my scruples, I crouched and drank the bitter water. The hollow was sheltered from the wind that had been sweeping endlessly against me as I traveled. I found a dry spot by the water's edge and stretched out to rest a moment. In my exhaustion the minute must have stretched into an hour. Something, some inner alarm, brought me to my senses.

Long shadows were stealing across the pond water and the light was turning red. One of those shadows, I thought dimly as I tried to move a sleep-stiffened elbow from under my head, seemed to be standing right over me. Drowsily I focused my sight and squinted against the declining sun. In the midst of the shadow I made out a very cold yellow eye and then saw that the thing looming over me was a great blue heron.

He was standing quietly on one foot and looking, like an expert rifleman, down the end of a bill as deadly as an assassin's dagger. I had seen, not long before, a man with his brow split open by a half-grown heron which he had been rash enough to try and capture. The man had been fortunate, for the inexperienced young bird had driven for his eye and missed, gashing his forehead instead.

The bird I faced was perfectly mature and had come softly down on a frog hunt while I slept. Why was he now standing over me? It was certain that momentarily he did not recognize me for a man. Perhaps he was merely curious. Perhaps it was only my little brown eye in the mud that he wanted. As this thought penetrated my sleeping brain I rolled, quick as a frog shrieking underfoot, into the water. The great bird, probably as startled as I, rose and beat steadily off into the wind, his long legs folded gracefully behind him.

A little shaken, I stood up and looked after him. There was nothing anywhere for miles and he had come to me like a ghost. How long he had been standing there I did not know. The light was dim now and the cold of the high plains was rising. I shivered and mopped my wet face. The snow on the peak was still visible. I got my bearings and hurried on, determined to make up for lost time. Again the long plain seemed to pass endlessly under my hastening footsteps. For hours I moved under the moon, not too disastrously, though once I fell. The sharp-edged arroyos had appeared again and were a menace in the dark. They were very hard to see, and some were deep.

It was some time after the moon rose that I began to realize that I was being followed. I stopped abruptly and listened. Something, several things, stopped with me. I heard their feet put down an instant after mine. Dead silence. "Who's there?" I said, trying to make the words adjustable and appeasing to any kind of unwanted companion. There was no answer, though I had the feel of several shapes just beyond my range of vision. There was nothing to do. I started on again and the footsteps began once more, but always they stopped and started with mine. Finally I began to suspect that the number of my stealthy followers was growing and that they were closing up the distance between us by degrees.

I had a choice then: I had been realizing it for some

time. I could lose my nerve, run, and invite pursuit, possibly breaking my leg in a ditch, or, like a sensible human being a little out of his element perhaps, I could go back and see what threatened me. On the instant, I stopped and turned.

There was a little clipclop of sound and dead silence once more, but this time I heard a low uneasy snuffling that could only come from many noses. I groped in the dark for a stick or a stone but could find none. I ran three steps back in a threatening manner and raised a dreadful screech that caused some shifting of feet and a little rumble of menacing sound. The screech had nearly shattered my own nerves. My heart thumped as I tried to recover my poise.

Cattle.

What was it that gave them this eerie behavior in the dark?

I affected to ignore them. I started on again, whistling, but my mouth was dry. Range cattle, something spelled out in my mind—wild, used to horsemen—what are they like to a man on foot in the dark? They were getting ominously close—that was certain; even if they were just curious, that steady trampling bearing down on my heels was nerve-wracking. Ahead of me at that instant I saw a section of barbed wire against the moon, and behind it a wide boulder-strewn stream bed.

The stream was dry and the starlight shone on the white stones. I swung about and yelled, making a little rush back. Then, without waiting to observe the effects, I turned and openly ran for it. There was a growing thunder behind me. I heard it as I vaulted the fence and landed eight feet down in the sand of the stream bed. Above me I heard a sound like a cavalry troop wheeling off into the night. A braver man might have stood by the fence and waited to see what would happen, but in the night there is this difference that comes over things. I sat on a stone in the stream bed and breathed hard for a long time. Then the chill forced me up again. The arroyo twisted in the direction I was headed. I wandered down it, feeling safer among the stones that reflected light and half-illuminated my path.

Somewhere along a section of damp sand I encountered several large toads who were also making a night journey and who hopped clumsily for a little way with me. There was something so attractive about their little bursts of energy that, tired as I was, I began to skip with them. I was delighted now to have even lowly company. First one would hop and then another, and I began to take my turn automatically with the rest. I do not know where they might have eventually led me, though I had a feeling that if I stayed and hopped with them long enough I might acquire this knowledge in some primordial manner.

With this thought I parted from them at a turn in the stream bed and made my way again over open rolling foothills in the dark. The land was rising. I was approaching the escarpment which I knew overhung the deeper valley in which lay the city at the mountain's foot.

I met nothing living now except small twisted pines. Boulders swelled up from the turf like huge white puff balls, and there was a flash of lightning off to the south that lit for one blue, glistening instant a hundred miles of churning, shifting landscape. I have thought since that each stone, each tree, each ravine and crevice echoing and re-echoing with thunder tells us more at such an instant than any daytime vision of the road we travel. The flash hangs like an immortal magnification in the brain, and suddenly you know the kind of country you pass over, and the powers abroad in it. It was at that moment that I reached the edge of the escarpment and looked down.

The night lights of the city glistened in hundreds far out on the plain, but I had chosen a bad pathway. I was high up on a clifflike eminence, and a straight descent in the dark was dangerous. As far as I could see there was no break to right or left. I was tired and hungry—too weary to go on circling in the dark and too cold to sit and wait for dawn. I decided to climb down, though with the utmost caution. Those faraway street lights beneath me were an irresistible attraction. They were the world I knew. The mind inside us is vaster than the world outside and I had been wrestling with its terrors for a long time now.

I began with discretion, working my way by inches down a precipitous gully. After a while the gully ended and I seemed to be looking out through a tree root at a solitary light on a mine tipple still far beneath me. I must have stayed there an hour groping about in the dark. Then I found a ledge along which I edged farther until I knocked over a stone that went rolling and grinding downward. Gaining momentum, it began to leap and volley against unseen stumps and boulders, making a hideous din.

As soon as the echoes died I knew I was in for trouble. I was well down from the summit now and there was no way back up that mountain wall in the dark. I heard them coming before I saw them—two huge watch dogs from the mine property. They barked with great night-foggy voices and leaped and slavered at me up the cliff. The sound was enough to wake the dead, and I expected at first that someone, a watchman, might appear. I hoped to be able to explain myself and have the man get the dogs under control. The dogs, however, happened to be alone. Nobody came and there I hung, a few feet up the cliff, while that formidable chorus played up and down my spine. The grip of my hands was growing tired and I thought with sudden careful prevision: If you wait till you're tired and fall, you won't be able to fight them off.

I climbed on then, slowly working downward along the ledge. I didn't want to have to drop suddenly in their midst. It would startle them, and if I were unlucky enough to fall they might spring on me. In fact, it looked as though they were going to spring in any case. But there it was. I tried to choose a moment when they seemed tired from their own great bellowing exertions. In a pause I vaulted down onto their own level from the wall.

I said something in a voice I tried to keep confident and friendly. I held one arm over my throat and stood stock-still. They came up to me warily, but one made a small woofing sound in his throat and I could see the motion of his tail in the dark. Seeing this, I dropped one hand on his head and the other on the other beast whose jaws had closed with surprising gentleness about my ankle. I stood there for long minutes talking and side-thumping and trying all the dog language I knew.

At the end of that time my foot was reluctantly released and the great hounds, with the total irrationality that prevails over the sheer cliff of Chaos, leaped and bounded about me, as though I were their returning master. Did they take me finally, because of my successful descent, as a demon like themselves—for, if I had fallen, they had given every indication of devouring me—or are the dogs of Cerberus, the hoarse-voiced, much feared guardian of Darkness, actually abysmally lonely and friendly creatures?

Since that long agonizing descent before I reached the city on the plain, I have never been quite sure. When I come to the Final Pit in which they howl, I shall, without too great a show of confidence, put out my hand and speak once more. Perhaps the great hounds of fear may wait with wagging tails for a voice which knows them. And what dog is there that knows how to tell one demon from another in the dark?

By the eyes, some will say, but I think not, really, for to the spectral tarsier in the bush, or to the owl in the churchyard tower, man and his lights must truly hold a demonic menace. Having journeyed once along the dark side of the planet, I am willing to testify that it is a shifting and unmapped domain of terrors. But as one demon to another, in memory of that hour on a cliff wall, I have helped a bat to escape from a university classroom, and I have never told on a frightened owl I once saw perched on the curtain rod above a Pullman berth. Somewhere in the blasts over the roaring cliff of Chaos I may meet their like again. It will be all one in that place, light and dark, big and small eyes, and the true demon will not fear his brother from another element. No. I think now the great dogs will know me. At least I shall put out my hand and speak.

4

INSTRUMENTS OF
DARKNESS

THE Nature in which Shakespeare's Macbeth dabbles so unsuccessfully with the aid of witchcraft, in the famous scene on the heath, is unforgettable in literature. We watch in horrified fascination the malevolent change in the character of Macbeth as he gains a dubious insight into the unfolding future—a future which we know to be self-created. This scene, fearsome enough at all times, is today almost unbearable to the discerning observer. Its power lies in its symbolic delineation of the relationship of Macbeth's midnight world to the realm of modern science—a relationship grasped by few.

The good general, Banquo, who, unlike Macbeth, is wary of such glimpses into the future as the witches have allowed the two companions, seeks to restrain his impetuous comrade. " 'Tis strange," Banquo says,

"And oftentimes, to winne us to our harme
    The Instruments of Darknesse tell us Truths
    Winne us with honest trifles, to betray's
    In deepest consequence."

Macbeth, who has immediately seized upon the self-imposed reality induced by the witches' prophecies, stumbles out of their toils at the last, only to protest in his dying hour:

"And Be these Jugling Fiends no more believ'd . . .
    That keep the word of promise to our eare,
    And breake it to our hope."

Who, we may now inquire, are these strange beings who waylaid Macbeth, and why do I, who have spent a lifetime in the domain of science, make the audacious claim that this old murderous tale of the scientific twilight extends its shadow across the doorway of our modern laboratories? These bearded, sexless creatures who possess the faculty of vanishing into air or who reappear in some ultimate flame-wreathed landscape only to mock our folly, are an exteriorized portion of ourselves. They are projections from our own psyche, smoking wisps of mental vapor that proclaim our subconscious intentions and bolster them with Delphic utterances—half-truths which we consciously accept, and which then take power over us. Under the spell of such oracles we create, not a necessary or real future, but a counterfeit drawn from within ourselves, which we then superimpose, through purely human power, upon reality. Indeed, one could say that these phantoms create a world that is at the same time spurious and genuine, so complex is our human destiny.

Every age has its style in these necromantic projections. The corpse-lifting divinations of the Elizabethan sorcerers have given way, in our time, to other and, at first sight, more scientific interpretations of the future. Today we know more about where man has come from and what we may expect of him—or so we think. But there is one thing which identifies Macbeth's "Jugling Fiends" in any age, whether these uncanny phantoms appear as witches, star readers, or today's technologists. This quality is their claim to omniscience—an omniscience only half stated on the basis of the past or specious present and always lacking in genuine knowledge of the future. The leading characteristic of the future they present is its fixed, static, inflexible quality.

Such a future is fated beyond human will to change, just as Macbeth's demons, by prophecy, worked in him a transformation of character which then created inevitable tragedy. Until the appearance of the witches on the heath gave it shape, that tragedy existed only as a latent possibility in Macbeth's subconscious. Similarly, in this age, one could quote those who seek control of man's destiny by the evocation of his past. Their wizardry is deceptive because their spells are woven out of a genuine portion of reality, which, however, has taken on this always identifiable quality of fixity in an unfixed universe. The ape is always in our hearts, we are made to say, although each time a child is born something totally and genetically unique enters the universe, just as it did long ago when the great ethical leaders—Christ, the Buddha, Confucius—spoke to their followers.

Man escapes definition even as the modern phantoms in militarist garb proclaim—as I have heard them do—that man will fight from one side of the solar system to the other, and beyond. The danger, of course, is truly there, but it is a danger which, while it lies partially in what man is, lies much more close to what he chooses to believe about himself. Man's whole history is one of transcendence and self-examination, which has led him to angelic heights of sacrifice as well as into the bleakest regions of despair. The future is not truly fixed but the world arena is smoking with the caldrons of those who would create tomorrow by evoking, rather than exorcising, the stalking ghosts of the past.

Even this past, however, has been far deeper and more pregnant with novelty than the short-time realist can envisage. As an evolutionist I never cease to be astounded by the past. It is replete with more features than one world can realize. Perhaps it was this that led the philosopher George Santayana to speak of men's true natures as not adequately manifested in their condition at any given moment, or even in their usual habits. "Their real nature," he contended, "is what they would discover themselves to be if they possessed self-knowledge, or as the Indian scripture has it, if they became what they are." I should like to approach this mystery of the self, which so intrigued the great philosopher, from a mundane path strewn with the sticks and stones through which the archaeologist must pick his way.

Let me use as illustration a very heavy and peculiar stone which I keep upon my desk. It has been split across and, carbon black, imprinted in the gray shale, is the outline of a fish. The chemicals that composed the fish—most of them at least—are still there in the stone. They are, in a sense, imperishable. They may come and go, pass in and out of living things, trickle away in the long erosion of time. They are inanimate, yet at one time they constituted a living creature.

Often at my desk, now, I sit contemplating the fish. Nor does it have to be a fish. It could be the long-horned Alaskan bison on my wall. For the point is, you see, that the fish is extinct and gone, just as those great heavy-headed beasts are gone, just as our massive-faced and shambling forebears of the Ice Age have vanished. The chemicals still about me here took a shape that will never be seen again so long as grass grows or the sun shines. Just once out of all time there was a pattern that we call *Bison regius,* a fish called *Diplomystus humilis*, and, at this present moment, a primate who knows, or thinks he knows, the entire score.

In the past there has been armor, there have been bellowings out of throats like iron furnaces, there have been phantom lights in the dark forest and toothed reptiles winging through the air. It has all been carbon and its compounds, the black stain running perpetually across the stone.

But though the elements are known, nothing in all those shapes is now returnable. No living chemist can shape a dinosaur; no living hand can start the dreaming tentacular extensions that characterize the life of the simplest ameboid cell. Finally, as the greatest mystery of all, I who write these words on paper, cannot establish my own reality. I am, by any reasonable and considered logic, dead. This may be a matter of concern, or even a secret, but if it is any consolation, I can assure you that all men are as dead as I. For on my office desk, to prove my words, is the fossil out of the stone, and there is the carbon of life stained black on the ancient rock.

There is no life in the fossil. There is no life in the carbon in my body. As the idea strikes me, and it comes as a profound shock, I run down the list of elements. There is no life in the iron, there is no life in the phosphorus, the nitrogen does not contain me, the water that soaks my tissues is not I. What am I then? I pinch my body in a kind of sudden desperation. My heart knocks, my fingers close around the pen. There is, it seems, a semblance of life here.

But the minute I start breaking this strange body down into its constituents, it is dead. It does not know me. Carbon does not speak, calcium does not remember, iron does not weep. Even if I hastily reconstitute their combinations in my mind, rebuild my arteries, and let oxygen in the grip of hemoglobin go hurrying through a thousand conduits, I have a kind of machine, but where in all this array of pipes and hurried flotsam is the dweller?

From whence, out of what steaming pools or boiling cloudbursts, did he first arise? What forces can we find which brought him up the shore, scaled his body into an antique, reptilian shape and then cracked it like an egg to let a soft-furred animal with a warmer heart emerge? And we? Would it not be a good thing if man were tapped gently like a fertile egg to see what might creep out? I sometimes think of this as I handle the thick-walled skulls of the animal men who preceded us or ponder over those remote splay-footed creatures whose bones lie deep in the world's wastelands at the very bottom of time.

With the glooms and night terrors of those vast cemeteries I have been long familiar. A precisely similar gloom enwraps the individual life of each of us. There are moments, in my bed at midnight, or watching the play of moonlight on the ceiling, when this ghostliness of myself comes home to me with appalling force, when I lie tense, listening as if removed, far off, to the footfalls of my own heart, or seeing my own head on the pillow turning restlessly with the round staring eyes of a gigantic owl. I whisper "Who?" to no one but myself in the silent, sleeping house—the living house gone back to sleep with the sleeping stones, the eternally sleeping chair, the picture that sleeps forever on the bureau, the dead, also sleeping, though they walk in my dreams. In the midst of all this dark, this void, this emptiness, I, more ghostly than a ghost, cry "Who? Who?" to no answer, aware only of other smaller ghosts like the bat sweeping by the window or the dog who, in repeating a bit of his own lost history, turns restlessly among nonexistent grasses before he subsides again upon the floor.

"Trust the divine animal who carries us through the world," writes Ralph Waldo Emerson. Like the horse who finds the way by instinct when the traveler is lost in the forest, so the divine within us, he contends, may find new passages opening into nature; human metamorphosis may be possible. Emerson wrote at a time when man still lived intimately with animals and pursued wild, dangerous ways through primeval forests and prairies. Emerson and Thoreau lived close enough to nature to know something still of animal intuition and wisdom. They had not reached that point of utter cynicism, that distrust of self and of the human past which leads finally to total entrapment in that past, "man crystallized," as Emerson again was shrewd enough to observe.

This entrapment is all too evident in the writings of many concerned with the evolutionary story of man. Their gaze is fixed solely upon a past into which, one begins to suspect, has been poured a certain amount of today's frustration, venom, and despair. Like the witches in *Macbeth*, these men are tempting us with seeming realities about ourselves until these realities take shape in our minds and become the future. It was not necessary to break the code of DNA in order to control human destiny. The tragedy lies in the fact that men are already controlling it even while they juggle retorts and shake vials in search of a physical means to enrich their personalities. We would like to contain the uncontainable future in a glass, have it crystallized out before us as a powder which we might swallow. All then, we imagine, would be well.

As our knowledge of the genetic mechanism increases, our ears are bombarded with ingenious accounts of how we are to control, henceforth, our own evolution. We who have recourse only to a past which we misread and which has made us cynics would now venture to produce our own future. Again I judge this self-esteem as a symptom of our time, our powerful misused technology, our desire not to seek the good life but to produce a painless mechanical version of it—our willingness to be good if goodness can, in short, be swallowed in a pill.

Once more we are on the heath of the witches, or, to come closer to our own day, we are in the London laboratory where the good Doctor Jekyll produced a potion and reft out of his own body the monster Hyde.

Nature, as I have tried to intimate, is never quite where we see it. It is a becoming as well as a passing, but the becoming is both within and without our power. This lesson, with all our hard-gained knowledge, is difficult to grasp. All along the evolutionary road it could have been said, "This is man," if there had then been such a magical self-delineating and mind-freezing word. It could have immobilized us at any step of our journey. It could have held us hanging to the bough from which we actually dropped; it could have kept us cowering, small-brained and helpless, whenever the great cats came through the reeds. It could have stricken us with terror before the fire that was later to be our warmth and weapon against ice-age cold. At any step of the way, the word "man," in retrospect, could be said to have encompassed just such final limits.

Each time the barrier has been surmounted. Man is not man. He is elsewhere. There is within us only that dark, divine animal engaged in a strange journey—that creature who, at midnight, knows its own ghostliness and senses its far road. "Man's unhappiness," brooded Thomas Carlyle, "comes of his Greatness; it is because there is an Infinite in him, which with all his cunning he cannot quite bring under the Finite." This is why hydrogen, which has become the demon element of our time, should be seen as the intangible dagger which hung before Macbeth's vision, but which had no power except what was lent to it by his own mind.

The terror that confronts our age is our own conception of ourselves. Above all else this is the potion which the modern Dr. Jekylls have concocted. As Shakespeare foresaw:

> "It hath been taught us from the primal state
> That he which is was wished until he were."

This is not the voice of the witches. It is the clear voice of a great poet almost four centuries gone, who saw at the dawn of the scientific age what was to be the darkest problem of man: his conception of himself. The words are quiet, almost cryptic; they do not foretell. They imply a problem in free will. Shakespeare, in this passage, says nothing of starry influences, machinery, beakers, or potions. He says, in essence, one thing only: that what we wish will come.

I submit that this is the deadliest message man will ever encounter in all literature. It thrusts upon him inescapable choices. Shakespeare's is the eternal, the true voice of the divine animal, piercing, as it has always pierced, the complacency of little centuries in which, encamped as in hidden thickets, men have sought to evade self-knowledge by describing themselves as men.

5

THE CHRESMOLOGUE

I

"FORMER men," observed Emerson in the dramatic days of the new geological science, "believed in magic, by which temples, cities and men were swallowed up, and all trace of them gone. We are coming on the secret of a magic which sweeps out of men's minds all vestige of theism and beliefs which they and their fathers held. . . . Nature," he contended clairvoyantly, "is a mutable cloud." Within that cloud is man. He constitutes in truth one of Emerson's most profound questions. Examined closely, he is more than a single puzzle. He is an indecipherable palimpsest, a walking document initialed and obscured by the scrawled testimony of a hundred ages. Across his features and written into the very texture of his bones are the half-effaced signatures of what he has been, of what he is, or of what he may become.

Modern man lives increasingly in the future and neglects the present. A people who seek to do this have an insatiable demand for soothsayers and oracles to assure and comfort them about the insubstantial road they tread. By contrast, I am a person known very largely, if at all, as one committed to the human past—to the broken columns of lost civilizations, to what can be discovered in the depths of tombs, or dredged from ice-age gravels, or drawn from the features of equally ancient crania. Yet as I go to and fro upon my scientific errands I find that the American public is rarely troubled about these antiquarian matters. Instead, people invariably ask, What will man be like a million years from now?—frequently leaning back with complacent confidence as though they already knew the answer but felt that the rituals of our society demanded an equally ritualistic response from a specialist. Or they inquire, as a corollary, what the scientists' views may be upon the colonization of outer space. In short, the cry goes up, Prophesy! Before attempting this dubious enterprise, however, I should like to recount the anecdote of a European philosopher who, over a hundred years ago, sensed the beginnings of the modern predicament.

It seems that along a particularly wild and forbidding section of the English coast—a place of moors, diverging and reconverging trackways, hedges, and all manner of unexpected cliffs and obstacles—two English gentlemen were out riding in the cool of the morning. As they rounded a turn in the road they saw a coach bearing down upon them at breakneck speed. The foaming, rearing horses were obviously running wild; the driver on the seat had lost the reins. As the coach thundered by, the terrified screams of the occupants could be heard.

The gentlemen halted their thoroughbred mounts and briefly exchanged glances. The same thought seemed to strike each at once. In an instant they set off at a mad gallop which quickly overtook and passed the lurching vehicle before them. On they galloped. They distanced it.

"Quick, the gate!" cried one as they raced up before a hedge. The nearest horseman leaped to the ground and flung wide the gate just as the coach pounded around the curve. As the swaying desperate driver and his equipage plunged through the opening, the man who had lifted the bar shouted to his companion, "Thirty guineas they go over the cliff!"

"Done!" cried his fellow, groping for his wallet.

The gate swung idly behind the vanished coach and the two sporting gentlemen listened minute by minute, clutching their purses. A bee droned idly in the heather and the smell of the sea came across the moor. No sound came up from below.

There is an odd resemblance in that hundred-year-old story to what we listen for today. We have just opened the gate and the purse is in our hands. The roads on that fierce coast diverge and reconverge. In some strange manner, in a single instant we are both the sporting gentlemen intent on their wager and the terrified occupants of the coach. There is no sound on all this wild upland. Something has happened or is about to happen, but what? The suspense is intolerable. We are literally enduring a future that has not yet culminated, that has perhaps been hovering in the air since man arose. The lunging, rocking juggernaut of our civilization has charged by. We wait by minutes, by decades, by centuries, for the crash we have engendered. The strain is in our minds and ears. The betting money never changes hands because there is no report of either safety or disaster. Perhaps the horses are still poised and falling on the great arc of the air.

We shift our feet uneasily and call to the first stranger for a word, a sanctified guess, an act of divination. As among the ancient Greeks, chresmologues, dealers in crumbling parchment and uncertain prophecy, pass among us. I am such a one. But the chresmologue's profession demands that he be alert to signs and portents in both the natural and human worlds—events or sayings that others might regard as trivial but to which the gods may have entrusted momentary meaning, pertinence, or power. Such words may be uttered by those unconscious of their significance, casually, as in a bit of overheard conversation between two men idling on a street, or in a bar at midnight. They may also be spoken upon journeys, for it is then that man in the role of the stranger must constantly confront reality and decide his pathway.

It was on such an occasion not long ago that I overheard a statement from a ragged derelict which would have been out of place in any age except, perhaps, that of the Roman twilight or our own time. A remark of this kind is one that a knowledgeable Greek would have examined for a god's hidden meaning and because of which a military commander, upon overhearing the words, might have postponed a crucial battle or recast his auguries.

I had come into the smoking compartment of a train at midnight, out of the tumult of a New York weekend. As I settled into a corner I noticed a man with a paper sack a few seats beyond me. He was meager of flesh and his cheeks had already taken on the molding of the skull beneath them. His threadbare clothing suggested that his remaining possessions were contained in the sack poised on his knees. His eyes were closed, his head flung back. He drowsed either from exhaustion or liquor, or both. In that city at midnight there were many like him.

By degrees the train filled and took its way into the dark. After a time the door opened and the conductor shouldered his way in, demanding tickets. I had one sleepy eye fastened on the dead-faced derelict. It is thus one hears from the gods.

"Tickets!" bawled the conductor.

I suppose everyone in the car was watching for the usual thing to occur. What happened was much more terrible.

Slowly the man opened his eyes, a dead man's eyes. Slowly a sticklike arm reached down and fumbled in his pocket, producing a roll of bills. "Give me," he said then, and his voice held the croak of a raven in a churchyard, "give me a ticket to wherever it is."

The conductor groped, stunned, over the bills. The dead eyes closed. The trainman's hastily produced list of stations had no effect. Obviously disliking this role of Charon he selected the price to Philadelphia, thrust the remaining bills into the derelict's indifferent hand, and departed. I looked around. People had returned to their papers, or were they only feigning?

In a single sentence that cadaverous individual had epitomized modern time as opposed to Christian time and in the same breath had pronounced the destination of the modern world. One of the most articulate philosophers of the twentieth century, Henri Bergson, has dwelt upon life's indeterminacy, the fact that it seizes upon the immobile, animates, organizes, and hurls it forward into time. In a single poignant expression this shabby creature on a midnight express train had personalized the terror of an open-ended universe. I know that all the way to Philadelphia I fumbled over my seat check and restudied it doubtfully. It no longer seemed to mean what it indicated. As I left the train I passed the bearer of the message. He slept on, the small brown sack held tightly in his lap. Somewhere down the line the scene would be endlessly repeated. Was he waiting for some final conductor to say, "This is the place," at a dark station? Or was there money in the paper sack and had he been traveling for a hundred years in these shabby coaches as a stellar object might similarly wander for ages on the high roads of the night?

All I can assert with confidence is that I was there. I

heard the destination asked for, I saw the money taken. I was professionally qualified to recognize an oracle when I heard one. It does not matter that the remark was cryptic. Good prophecy is always given in riddles, for the gods do not reveal their every secret to men. They only open a way and wait for mortal nobility or depravity to take its natural course. "A ticket to wherever it is" carries in the phrase itself the weight of a moral judgment. No civilization professes openly to be unable to declare its destination. In an age like our own, however, there comes a time when individuals in increasing numbers unconsciously seek direction and taste despair. It is then that dead men give back answers and the sense of confusion grows. Soothsayers, like flies, multiply in periods of social chaos. Moreover, let us not confuse ourselves with archaic words. In an age of science the scientist may emerge as a soothsayer.

II

There is one profound difference which separates psychologically the mind of the classical world from that of the present: the conception of time. The Ancient World was, to use Frank Manuel's phrase, bound to the wheel of Ixion, to the maxim: what has been is, passes, and will be. By contrast, the Christian thinkers of Western Europe have, until recently, assumed a short time scale of a few millennia. In addition, Christianity replaced the cyclical recurrences of Greek and Roman history by the concept of an unreturning past. History became the drama of the Fall and the Redemption, and therefore, as drama, was forewritten and unrepeatable. Novelty was its essence, just as duration and repetition lay at the heart of classical thinking.

Between the earlier conception of time and its reordering in the phrase, what is will *not* be, lies an ir-

redeemable break with the past even though, in the course
of two thousand years, much has changed and conceptions
derived originally from both realms of thought have inter-
penetrated. Western philosophy has been altered under
the impact of science and become secularized, but history
as the eternally new, as "progress," repeats the millenari-
anism of Christianity. As for the time scale, which modern
science has enormously extended, the intuitions of the ancients have proved correct, but biology has contributed an
unreturning novelty to the shapes of life. Thus the great
play has lengthened and become subject to the mysterious
contingencies which are the proper matter of genetics. The
play itself remains, however, just as the anthropologist has
similarly demonstrated in the social realm, a performance
increasingly strange, diverse, and unreturning. In the light
of this distinction, the role of the oracle in the ancient
world can be seen to differ from that of his modern ana-
logue, whether the latter be disguised as a science-fiction
writer, a speculative scientist engaged in rational extrapo-
lation, or a flying-saucer enthusiast replacing the out-
moded concept of the guardian angel by the guarding intelligence of extraterrestrial beings.

Since emergent creativity went largely unnoticed in the
living world, the kind of future in which Western man
now participates was also neglected. Men lived amidst the
ruins of past civilizations or epochs, indifferently wedging
great sculpture or invaluable inscriptions into the wall of a
peasant's hut or a sheep corral. Few indeed were the attempts to probe the far future or the remote past. Men re-
quested of the oracles what men have always desired: the
cure for illness, the outcome of battle, the wisdom or un-
wisdom of a sea journey, the way to a girl's heart. They
asked, in effect, next day's or next year's future because,
save for the misfortunes that beset the individual's pathway, all lives and all generations were essentially the
same.

There was, in the words of the Old Testament, "nothing new under the sun." The wind went about its circuits; the wave subsided on the beach only to rise again. The generations of men were like the wave—endless but the same. It was a wave of microcosmic futures, the difference between the emperor in purple and the slave under the lash. Each man was mortal; roles could be reversed and sometimes were. This was important to the buffeted individual but not to the wave. Men's individual fates resembled the little dance of particles under the microscope that we call the Brownian movement.

Perhaps, over vaster ranges of time than man has yet endured, the dance of civilizations may seem as insignificant. Indeed it must have seemed so intuitively to the ancients, for, in the endless rising and falling of the wave, lost palace and lost throne would all come round again. It was of little use, therefore, to trouble one's heart over the indecipherable inscription on a fallen monument. Let the immortal gods on the mountain keep their own accounts. In the sharp cold of midwinter one asked only if next year's pastures would be green.

But with the agony in the garden at Gethsemane came the concern for last things, for the end of the story of man. A solitary individual, one who prayed sleepless that his fate might pass, had spoken before the Pharisees, "I know whence I have come and whither I am going." No man had said such a thing before and none would do so after him. For our purpose here it does not matter what we believe or disbelieve; whether we are pagan, Jew, Christian, or Marxist. The voice and the words were those of a world-changer.

At the place Golgotha they say the earth shook. It is true in retrospect, for the mind of Western man was there shaken to its foundations. It had gained the courage to ask the final terrible question: for what end was it made? Not the insignificant queries long addressed to wandering magicians, but such a question as a man could ask only in a desert: What is the end? Not of me, not of my neighbor or my generation, but the end of man. For what was the lime engendered in our bones, our bodies made to rise in the bright sun and again in dust to be laid down? It may well be that rocks were torn when that cry escaped on human breath. With it man had entered unknowingly upon history, upon limitless time, and equally limitless change. Nothing would be what it had been. The wave would fall no longer idly on the shore. It would loom vaster, bluer, darker until lightning played along its summit, the deepest, most dangerous wave in the entire universe—the wave of man.

The play upon which man had entered would at first be confined to a tiny immovable stage. Its acts would be centered within the brief time span then humanly conceivable. The very compression and foreshortening thus achieved, however, would heighten the intensity of the drama and whet man's concern with the unique course of events. The ancient cyclical conceptions of the pagan world would seem wearisome and banal, its gods without dignity. By contrast, a historic event, the mallet strokes upon a hill outside Jerusalem, would echo in men's minds across nineteen hundred years.

The Crucifixion was not an act that could be re-endured perpetually. "God forbid," wrote Saint Augustine, "that we should believe this. Christ died once for our sins, and, rising again, dies no more." The magnitude of the universe remained unknown, its time depths undiscovered, its evolutionary transformations unguessed. One thing alone had changed: the drama of man's life. It now had force, direction, and significance beyond the purely episodic. The power of a single divinity sustained the stage, the drama, and the actors. Men had arrived at true historicity. Acts of evil and of good would run long shadows out into eternity. Self-examination and self-knowledge would be intensified.

On this scene of increasing cosmic order would also emerge eventually a heightened interest in nature as a manifestation of that same divinity. In time, nature would be spoken of as the second look of God's revelation. Some would regard it as the most direct communication of all, less trammeled by words, less obscured by human contention. There would begin, by degrees, the attentive, innocent examination that would lead on through doubts and questionings to the chill reality of the ever-wandering stars, to time stretched across millions of light-years, or read in the erosion of mountain systems or by virtue of unexpected apparitions in the stratified rocks. Finally, Jean Baptiste Lamarck, in 1809, the year of Darwin's birth, would venture dryly, "Doubtless nothing exists but the will of the sublime Author of all things, but can we set rules for him in the execution of his will, or fix the routine for him to observe? Could not his infinite power create an order of things which gave existence *successively* to all that we see . . . ?"

The tragedy on a barren hill in Judea, which for so long had held human attention, would seem to shrink to a minuscule event on a sand-grain planet lost in a whirl of fiery galaxies. Reluctantly men would peer into the hollow eye sockets of the beasts from which they had sprung. The Christian dream would linger but the surety of direction would depart. Nature, the second book of the theologians, would prove even more difficult of interpretation than the first. Once launched upon the road into the past, man's insatiable hunger to devour eternity would grow. He would seek to live in past, present, and future as one, one eternity of which he might be the intellectual master.

Over fifty years ago it was possible to catch something of this feeling in the musings of the archaeologist Arthur Weigall, wandering in the upper Egyptian deserts. In an abandoned quarry he came upon many hewn stones addressed, as he says, "to the Caesars, but never dispatched to them; nor is there anything in this time-forsaken valley which so brings the past before one as do these blocks awaiting removal to vanished cities. . . . Presently," he continues, "a door seems to open in the brain. Two thousand years have the value of the merest drop of water."

III

Like Weigall, the desert wanderer, I have done much walking in my younger years. When I climbed I almost always carried seeds with me in my pocket. Often I liked to carry sunflower seeds, acorns, or any queer "sticktight" that had a way of gripping fur or boot tops as if it had an eye on Himalayas and meant to use the intelligence of others to arrive at them. I have carried such seeds up the sheer walls of mesas and I have never had illusions that I was any different to them from a grizzly's back or a puma's paw.

They had no interest in us, bear, panther, or man—but they were endowed with a preternatural knowledge that at some point we would lie down and there they would start to grow. I have, however, aided their machinations in a way they could scarcely have intended. I have dropped sunflower seed on stony mesa tops and planted cactus in alpine meadows amidst the sounds of water and within sight of nodding bluebells. I have sowed northern seeds south and southern seeds north and crammed acorns into the most unlikely places. You can call it a hobby if you like. In a small way I, too, am a world-changer and hopefully tampering with the planetary axis. Most of my experiments with the future will come to nothing but some may not.

Life is never fixed and stable. It is always mercurial, rolling and splitting, disappearing and re-emerging in a most unpredictable fashion. I never make a journey to a wood or a mountain without experiencing the temptation to explode a puffball in a new clearing or stopping to encourage some sleepy monster that is just cracking out of the earth mold. This is, of course, an irresponsible attitude, since I cannot tell what will come of it, but if the world hangs on such matters it may be well to act boldly and realize all immanent possibilities at once. Shake the seeds out of their pods, I say, launch the milkweed down, and set the lizards scuttling. We are in a creative universe. Let us then create. After all, man himself is the unlikely consequence of such forces. In the spring when a breath of wind sets the propellers of the maple seeds to whirring, I always say to myself hopefully, "After us the dragons."

To have dragons one must have change; that is the first principle of dragon lore. Otherwise everything becomes stale, commonplace, and observed. I suspect that it is this unimaginative boredom that leads to the vulgar comment that evolution may be all very well as a theory but you can never really see anything in the process of change. There is also the even more obtuse and less defensible attitude of those who speak of the world's creative energies as being exhausted, the animals small and showing no significant signs of advance. "Everything is specialized in blind channels," some observers contend. "Life is now locked permanently in little roadside pools, or perching dolefully on television aerials."

Such men never pause to think how *they* might have looked gasping fishily through mats of green algae in the Devonian swamps, but that is where the *homunculus* who preceded them had his abode. I have never lost a reverent and profound respect for swamps, even individually induced ones. I remember too well what, on occasion, has come out of them. Only a purblind concern with the present can so limit men's views, and it is my contention that a sympathetic observer, even at this moment, can witness such marvels of transitional behavior, such hoverings between the then and the now, as to lay forever to rest the notion that evolution belongs somewhere in the witch world of the past.

One may learn much in those great cemeteries of which Weigall spoke, those desolate Gobis and wind-etched pinnacles that project like monuments out of the waste of time itself. One must learn, however, to balance their weight of shards and bones against a frog's leap, against a crow's voice, against a squeak in the night or something that rustles the foliage and is gone. It is here that the deception lies. The living are never seen like the dead and the living appear to be so surely what they are. We lack the penetration to see the present and the onrushing future contending for the soft feathers of a flying bird, or a beetle's armor, or shaking painfully the frail confines of the human heart.

We are in the center of the storm and we have lost our sense of direction. It is not out of sadistic malice that I have carried cockleburs out of their orbit or blown puffball smoke into new worlds. I wanted to see to what vicissitudes they might adapt or in what mountain meadows the old thorns might pass away. One out of all those seeds may grope forward into the future and writhe out of its current shape. It is similarly so on the windswept uplands of the human mind.

Evolution is far more a part of the unrolling future than it is of the past, for the past, being past, is determined and done. The present, in the words of Karl Heim, "is still in the molten phase of becoming. It is still undecided. It is still being fought for." The man who cannot perceive that battleground looks vaguely at some animal which he expects to transform itself before his eyes. When it does not, he shrugs and says, "Evolution is all very well but you cannot see it. Besides it does not direct you. It only teaches you that you are an animal and had better act like one."

Yet even now the thing we are trying to see is manifesting itself. Missing links, partial adaptations, transitions from one environmental world to another, animals caught in slow motion half through some natural barrier are all about us. They literally clamor for our attention. We ourselves are changelings. Like Newton, those who possess the inclination and the vision may play on the vast shores of the universe with the living seeds of future worlds. Who knows, through the course of unimaginable eons, how the great living web may vibrate slightly and give out a note from the hand that plucked it long ago? In the waste dumps at city edges bloom plants that have changed and marched with man across the ages since he sat by hill barrows and munched with the dogs. A hand there, brown with sun, threw a seed and the world altered. Perhaps, in some far meadow, a plant of mine will survive the onset of an age of ice. Perhaps my careless act will root life more firmly in the dying planetary days when man is gone and the last seeds shower gallantly against the frost.

What is true biologically is also true along the peripheries of the mind itself. We possess our own alpine meadows, excoriating heat, and freezing cold. There have been, according to philosophers, political man, religious man, economic man. Today there are, variously, psychological man, technological man, scientific man. Dropped seeds, all of them, the mind's response to its environments, its defense against satiety. He who seeks naïvely to embrace his own time will accept its masks and illusions. The men of one period may turn completely to religious self-examination and become dogmatically contentious. Our own age, by contrast, turns outward, as if in the flight from self of which its rockets have become the symbol. It has been well said by Philip Rieff that every personality cure seems to expose man to a new illness. I believe it is because man always chooses to rest on his cure.

We have forgotten the greatest injunction of the wise traveler from Galilee. He did not say before the Pharisees, "I know where I am *staying*." Instead he observed that he knew where he was going. As is true of all great prophets, he left something unspoken hanging in the air. Men have chosen to assume that Jesus had knowledge of his physical fate or that he was bound to some safe haven beyond mortal reach. It seldom occurs to us that he was definitely engaged on a journey. If, in traveling that road, it led incidentally to a high place called Golgotha, it was because his inward journey was higher and more dangerous still.

Five centuries ago an unknown Christian mystic spoke thus of heaven, which his contemporaries assumed to be a definable place: "Heaven ghostly, is as high down as up, and up as down: behind as before, before as behind, on one side as another. Insomuch, that whoso had a true desire for to be at heaven, then that same time he were in heaven ghostly. For the high and the next way thither is run by desires and not by paces of feet."

Today our glimpses of heaven have become time-projected. They are secular; they are translated into paces measured by decades and centuries. Science is the assumed instrument and progress a dynamic flow, as is the heaven we seek to create or abjure. In final analysis we deceive ourselves. Our very thought, through the experimental method, is outwardly projected upon time and space until it threatens to lose itself, unexamined, in vast distances. It does not perform the contemplative task of inward perception.

The mysterious author of *The Cloud of Unknowing* spoke rightly and his words apply equally to that future we seek to conjure up. The future is neither ahead nor behind, on one side or another. Nor is it dark or light. It is contained within ourselves; it is drawn from ourselves; its evil and its good are perpetually within us. The future that we seek from oracles, whether it be war or peace, starvation or plenty, disaster or happiness, is not forward to be come upon. Rather its gestation is now, and from the confrontation of that terrible immediacy we turn away to spatial adventures and to imagination projected into time as though the future were fixed, unmalleable to the human will, and to be come upon only as a seventeenth-century voyager might descry, through his spyglass, smoke rising from an unknown isle.

Not so is the human future. It is made of stuff more immediate and inescapable—ourselves. If our thought runs solely outward and away upon the clever vehicles of science, just so will there be in that future the sure intellectual impoverishment and opportunism which flight and anonymity so readily induce. It will be, and this is the difficult obstacle of our semantics, not a future come upon by accident with all its lights and shadows, guiltless, as in a foreign sea. It will be instead the product of our errors, hesitations, and escapes, returning inexorably as the future which we wished only to come upon like a geographical discoverer, but to have taken no responsibility in shaping.

If, therefore, it is my occasional task to cast auguries, I will add as pertinent some further words of that long-vanished seer: "Be wary that thou conceive not bodily, that which is meant ghostly, although it be spoken bodily in bodily words as be these, up or down, in or out, behind or before. This thought may be better felt than seen; for it is full blind and full dark to them that have but little while looked thereupon." If we banish this act of contemplation and contrition from our midst, then even now we are dead men and the future dead with us. For the endurable future is a product not solely of the experimental method, or of outward knowledge alone. It is born of compassion. It is born of inward seeing. The unknown one called it simply "All," and he added that it was not in a bodily manner to be wrought.

IV

A former colleague of mine, who was much preoccupied with travel and who suffered from absent-mindedness, once turned timidly to his wife as he set forth upon a long journey. "Is the place where I am going," he asked her anxiously, for he depended much upon her notes of instruction, "in my pocket?" It strikes me now that in few centuries has the way seemed darker or the maps we carry in our separate pockets more contradictory, if not indecipherable.

The Russians in their early penetration of space saw fit to observe irreverently that they had not seen heaven or glimpsed the face of God. As for the Americans, in our first effort we could only clamorously exclaim, "Boy, what a ride!" During those words on a newscast I had opened a window on the night air. It was moonrise. In spite of the cynical Russian pronouncement, my small nephew had just told me solemnly that he had seen God out walking. Concerned as adults always are lest children see something best left unseen, I consulted his mother. She thought a moment. Then a smile lighted her face. "I told him God made the sun and the stars," she explained. "Now he thinks the moon is God."

I went and reasoned gravely with him. The gist of my extemporized remarks came from the medieval seer. "Not up, or down," I cautioned, "nor walking in the sun, nor in the night—above all not that."

There was a moment of deep concentration. An uncertain childish voice reached up to me suddenly. "Then where did God get all the dirt?"

I, in my turn, grew quiet and considered.

"Out of a dark hat in a closet called Night," I parried. "We, too, come from there."

"*Conceive it better as not wrought by hands,*" the voice repeated in my head.

"Then how do we see Him?" the dubious little voice trailed up to me. "Where is He then?"

"He is better felt than seen," I repeated. "We do not look up or down but in here." I touched the boy's heart lightly. "In here is what a great man called simply 'All.'

The rest is out there"—I gestured—"and roundabout. It is not nearly so important."

The world was suddenly full of a vast silence. Then upon my ear came a sound of galloping, infinitely remote, as though a great coach passed, sustained upon the air. I touched the child's head gently. "We are in something called a civilization," I said, "a kind of wagon with horses. It is running over the black bridge of nothing. If it falls, we fall."

"Thirty guineas," a cricket voice chirped in my brain. I shut it out along with the glimpse of a sea cliff in the English fog.

"Conceive it not bodily," the clear voice persisted like a bell, "for it is meant ghostly." From below a hand gave itself up trustingly to mine.

"I saw Him. I did so," said the child.

"We will go and look all about," I comforted, "for that is good to do. But mostly we will look inside, for that is where we ache and where we laugh and where at last we die. I think it is mostly there that He is very close."

We went out side by side a little shyly onto the lawn and watched the stars. After a while, and carefully, being small, we turned and looked for the first time at our two selves. Not bodily, I mean, but ghostly. And being still the wandering chresmologue, I told him about a very ancient manuscript in which is dimly written: "Wherever thou wilt thou dost assemble me, and in assembling me thou dost assemble thyself."

6

PAW MARKS AND BURIED TOWNS

M ANY years ago, when the first cement sidewalks were being laid in our neighborhood, we children took the paw of our dog Mickey and impressed it into a kind of immortality even as he modestly floundered and objected. Some time ago after the lapse of many decades, I stood and looked at the walk, now crumbling at the edges from the feet of many passers.

No one knows where Mickey the friendly lies; no one knows how many times the dust that clothed that beautiful and loving spirit has moved with the thistledown across the yards where Mickey used to play. Here is his only legacy to the future—that dabbled paw mark whose secret is remembered briefly in the heart of an aging professor.

The mark of Mickey's paw is dearer to me than many more impressive monuments—perhaps because, in a sense, we both wanted to be something other than what we were. Mickey, I know, wanted very much to be a genuine human being. If permitted, he would sit up to the table and put his paws together before his plate, like the rest of the children. If anyone mocked him at such a time by pretending to have paws and resting his chin on the table as Mickey had to do, Mickey would growl and lift his lip. He knew very well he was being mocked for not being human.

The reminder that he was only a poor dog with paws annoyed Mickey. He knew basically a lot more than he ever had the opportunity to express. Though people refused to take Mickey's ambition seriously, the frustration never affected his temperament. Being of a philosophic cast of mind, he knew that children were less severe in their classifications. And if Mickey found the social restrictions too onerous to enable him quite to achieve recognition inside the house, outside he came very close to being a small boy. In fact, he was taken into a secret order we had founded whose club house was an old piano box in the backyard. We children never let the fact that Mickey walked on four legs blind us to his other virtues.

Now the moral of all this is that Mickey tried hard to be a human being. And as I stood after the lapse of years and looked at the faint impression of his paw, it struck me that every ruined civilization is, in a sense, the mark of men trying to be human, trying to transcend themselves. Like Mickey, none of them has quite made it, but they have each left a figurative paw mark—the Shang bronzes, the dreaming stone faces on Easter Island, the Parthenon, the Sphinx, or perhaps only rusted stilettos, chain mail, or a dolmen on some sea-pounded headland. The archaeologist, it is said, is a student of the artifact. That harsh, unlovely word, as sharply angled as a fist ax or a brick, denudes us of human sympathy. In the eye of the public we loom, I suppose, as slightly befuddled graybeards scavenging in grave heaps. We caw like crows over a bit of jade or broken potsherd: we are eternally associated in the public mind with sharp-edged flints and broken statues. The utter uselessness of the past is somehow magnificently incorporated into our activities.

No one, I suppose, would believe that an archaeologist is a man who knows where last year's lace valentines have gone, or that from the surface of rubbish heaps the thin and ghostly essence of things human keeps rising through the centuries until the plaintive murmur of dead men and women may take precedence at times over the living voice. A man who has once looked with the archaeological eye will never see quite normally. He will be wounded by what other men call trifles. It is possible to refine the sense of time until an old shoe in the bunch grass or a pile of nineteenth-century beer bottles in an abandoned mining town tolls in one's head like a hall clock. This is the price one pays for learning to read time from surfaces other than an illuminated dial. It is the melancholy secret of the artifact, the humanly touched thing.

Although the successful moon rockets have swung everyone's attention to outer space, a surprising number of archaeological books dealing with the lost city civilizations are still being published. The rapidity of their appearance and the avidity with which they are received suggest that while the public's eye has been forced upward it has also, in the same act, been cast downward toward the earth. Perhaps no great civilization ever before has been more self-consciously aware of the possible doom that confronts it or more curious about those brother thinkers and artists who carved the gods that lie now in temples visited by rain, or who ventured through the Pillars of Hercules when all beyond was wild and unknown as outer space is today. They built in their separate ways, then fell, and we, with one winged foot poised toward the stars, hear in a subdued quiet the old voices out of the grass. Whatever the disease that ate the heart of these lost cultures it was not the affliction of ignorance—not, at least, the technical ignorance of the savage who cannot lay one stone successfully upon another. In every one of the fallen cities which our spades have revealed, there existed the clever artisan, the engineer devoted to the service of the particular human dream that flourished there.

Here is Leonard Cottrell's description of the Ceylonese city of Annadhapura, known to be roughly contemporaneous, in the West, with the conquests of Alexander the Great:

". . . the palaces . . . would have made Diocletian's palace seem a poor thing by comparison, their great *dagobas*, artificial hills of masonry supporting shrines and reliquaries, were sometimes over three hundred feet high, and can be compared with the pyramids of Egypt. Their hydraulic engineering has no parallel save in the nineteenth and twentieth centuries; for example, the artificial lake of Mineria, created in the third century A.D. by Maha Sen, has a circumference of twenty miles, and the masonry and earthwork dams which were made to divert the waters of the stream which fills it extend for eighty miles; their average height is eighty feet."

Today, in the ruined tanks of those great Sinhalese cities, the bear alone stands upright, and leopards drink from the few puddles that remain. The cunning workers in stone and gold have long since departed. Given time enough, this is a state of affairs more the rule than the exception among the cities of men, as the studies of the modern urban archaeologists clearly demonstrate. The lesson is felt in the search for a single burial, as in *The Lost Pyramid* by the late Egyptian archaeologist Zakaria Goneim. The story of Goneim's excavation, ending in the presence of a mysterious alabaster coffin of an unknown third dynasty pharaoh, is a peculiarly fascinating one. The coffin he discovered proved to be totally empty, although a wreath had been laid upon it before it was left in the darkness of its burial vault almost five thousand years ago. The evidence did not suggest the usual tomb robbery, but rather some bit of human drama lost forever in the darkness that shrouds the history of the Old Kingdom. Dr. Goneim, moreover, was not ashamed to acknowledge the feelings of which I have earlier spoken—the increasing sensitivity of the archaeologist to the voices from the ground:

"No one who has not crawled along the galleries beneath a pyramid, and experienced the silence and darkness, can fully appreciate the sensation which, at times, overwhelms one. It may sound fantastic, but I felt that the pyramid had a personality and that this personality was that of the king for whom it was built and which still lingered within it. I know that my workmen, some of whom have spent their whole lives in such work, often experience this feeling. You crawl along some dark corridor on hands and knees, past falls of rock; the light of the lamp gleams on minute crystals in the stratified walls; beyond, the corridor disappears into the blackness. You turn corners, feeling your way with your hands; the workmen have been left behind, and suddenly you realize you are alone in a place which has not heard a footfall for nearly fifty centuries."

After this, the individual vicariously devoted to archaeological adventure is only too eager to wander among the lost cities and buried libraries of Babylonia or to follow spirited accounts of ancient Egypt, including the still fascinating though often-told story of the Tutankhamen discovery. Perhaps, in the end, part of the pathos which the episode holds for us rests in the youth of that young king interred in April, left with a wreath of cornflowers on his breast, to lie alone for three thousand years encased in solid gold.

One may now have a choice of cities like Pompeii, destroyed by the elements, or cities stricken down by war, or cities ruined by the vagaries of trade. Mohenjo-daro and Harappa, whose writing no man can read, perhaps passed to their end by conquest. Today the carefully laid out cities lie in a waste of sand.

The North African cities of Sabratha and Leptis Magna, since they have been extensively photographed, touch us more closely. In these photographs we come back to what I spoke of as the artifact, the humanly touched thing. Here, in a series of clear, sunlit pictures, remnants of the Roman civilization, once as powerful as our own, are seen dissolving under sand and wind. From Libya there came the vast quantities of wheat and olive oil that nourished metropolitan Rome. Now the theaters lie empty and open to the sun, and the baths are waterless; but still the bold Roman letters stand across the entrance to the theater at Leptis Magna, naming, amid the surrounding ruin, one Annobal, the donor.

The columns totter; Annobal has left a paw mark and gone thence, like my dog Mickey. It is the immediacy, across the waste of centuries, that catches the heart—the sculptured head that might have just been finished in a modern studio, the empty seats vacated by a crowd that has just left but is not coming back. As I study such pictures I am reminded of a feeling I once experienced when examining a remarkable Victorian photograph of a girl waif asleep on a London park bench. She was obviously poor, her shoes were scuffed, her young body ill at ease in its graceless Victorian garments. There was despair and beauty in her face—so much beauty that it was like looking through a little window in time and wanting to reach out and touch her shoulder in compassion. I realized with difficulty that I was glancing for one unrelieved instant upon a drama ended before I was born, a drama and a human soul upon whom I would never look again. Where she went upon the evening of that day a century ago or what darkness swallowed her up, it would never be mine to know. Now, looking once more upon the ruined Roman theater, it comes to me that not even the shadow of a shadow remains of the good citizen Annobal. Even worse, the roofs of the town he loved, and to whose arts he contributed, lie open to the stars.

I have said that the ruins of every civilization are the marks of men trying to express themselves, to leave an impression upon the earth. We in the modern world have turned more stones, listened to more buried voices, than any culture before us. There should be a kind of pity that comes with time, when one grows truly conscious and looks behind as well as forward, for nothing is more brutally savage than the man who is not aware he is a shadow. Nothing is more real than the real; and that is why it is well for men to hurt themselves with the past—it is one road to tolerance.

The long history of man, besides its enobling features, contains also a disruptive malice which continues into the present. Since the rise of the first neolithic cultures, man has hanged, tortured, burned, and impaled his fellow men. He has done so while devoutly professing religions whose founders enjoined the very opposite upon their followers. It is as though we carried with us from some dark tree in a vanished forest, an insatiable thirst for cruelty. Of all the wounds man's bodily organization has suffered in his achievement of a thinking brain, this wound is the most grievous of all, this shadow of madness, which has haunted every human advance since the dawn of history and which may well precipitate the final episode in the existence of the race.

Not many months ago I chanced to be lecturing at a

university whose grounds adjoin a depressed area of slums.
After the conclusion of the class hour I sauntered out into
a courtyard filled with sunshine and some fragments of
Greek statuary. As I passed by the inner gate I was confronted by a scene as old as time. Approaching me along
the path upon which they had intruded by squirming
through a hedge, was a ragged band of children led by a
sharp-featured boy with a bow. The arrow he held drawn
was pointed with tin. Instinctively we both paused—I because I feared for my eyes. There was no more human recognition in the face of the leader than I might have received from a group of hunting man-apes on the African
savanna. We measured each other as mutually powerful
and unknown forces, best to be avoided. The band drew
in unconsciously about its leader and veered aside, with
that wide, momentary animal stare haunting me as they
passed. Before my eyes there marched a million years of
human history, and I was a stranger and afraid, although,
in my own lifetime, I had made that formidable passage
from the caves and sewers of my childhood to this deceptively quiet campus across which these ghosts of long ago
now persisted in passing. There was no humor in them, no
real play. They slunk on, cruel as man's past, deadly, with
the bow poised and the sharp, observant eyes alert to spy
out any helpless thing.

I sighed with relief as they clambered over an embank-
ment and disappeared. On a nearby bench with my books
spread out before me I did not read. "Man will survive," I
said to myself, touched with a slight horror. "God should
pity the world. Man will survive." All that passionate energy which in my own life, after many stumblings, had
lodged me in these great silent halls, suddenly seemed dis-
sipated and lost. I was as empty and filled with light as a
milkweed pod whose substance has evaporated into the silvery autumn air. I thought of the beautiful ruined courts
of an Aztec city in which I once had stood. I drew my

hand over the bust of Hermes that I knew with surety would find a second burial in the earth. More ghostly, more insubstantial than that hunting pack which roams the world and its dark thickets forever, I felt the dissolving power of the light which falls across lost columns and bleaching mosaics. Beauty man has, but in the very act of possession he is dissolved. I saw in my hand against the statue the projected shriveling of the skin. Each man repeats that history—endlessly and forever.

Nor has any civilization sustained beauty without returning it to the earth. But perhaps man will eventually achieve this victory, I thought doubtfully, standing a little longer in the timeless eternal light that flowed from the great sculpture. Perhaps. Perhaps he will, I thought again, and went on my way toward the darkness.

7

BARBED WIRE AND BROWN SKULLS

I

ARCHAEOLOGISTS, during the course of their lives, see and hear many strange things, but the fact that they are scientific men keeps them for the most part silent. They have good, if not superior, rationalizations for the things they do. No layman would dare impugn their motives. I, for example, have a certain number of skulls in my possession. As I write I can see four on the shelf above me. At least two are hidden in my filing cabinet, and there is a beautiful fragment on my desk which is often fondled by visitors who are unaware of its human significance.

Now as it happens I am fortunate. I practice a trade which enables me to keep these objects about in a perfectly logical and open manner. I have not murdered to possess them, and if one or two were acquired in dark and musty places, my motives, as I have hinted, are beyond reproach. As an archaeologist I can be both a good citizen and a frequenter of graveyards.

It was different in the case of the man who finally led me to question my own motives as a skull collector. He was a lawyer, but that, perhaps, has little to do with the tale. I knew him as an austere, high-collared member of the bar—a moral and upright citizen—but that, I am afraid, has little to do with it either. The truth is that the gentleman left a box.

He had died, and after the passage of a certain number of months during which the box either lay undiscovered in his attic or, as is more likely, circulated uneasily through the hands of his heirs, I received a call about it. There was nothing unusual in this. I was simply not a policeman. When you are the heir to a considerable estate and unfortunately also have a box to be disposed of, you never go to a policeman. You go instead to an archaeologist. He is apt to be more understanding of human frailty, less prone to dark suspicions than a police officer, and above all, he will relieve you of the box.

If you have ever wandered the streets of a strange city with a parcel of this nature, you will appreciate the fact that there are very few human beings who can be trusted to relieve you of such a burden without making some hideous public commotion. Naturally you wish to avoid this. There are only two solutions: bury the box (an act which can lead to serious complications, including the suggestion of guilt) or find an archaeologist, smiling trustingly, and deposit it in his arms.

The heirs in this case pursued the inevitable pathway. They came to me. The legal gentleman and I had had mutual friends. My profession was known. Perhaps the property was really mine. Attics, you know, and the things that get into them. A loan perhaps? Some lodge doings?

I reserved a noncommittal air.

"Uncle Tobias was a church man. He would not tolerate—"

Yes, I said, I knew that.

A nephew toyed uneasily with the strings of the box. "It is very unlikely that his profession would have brought him into contact with—?"

"And him a lawyer?" I said. "Nothing likelier."

The niece's hands twisted. "Show him," she prompted.

It was the real thing, of course, and no lodge fake. As fine a skull as I've ever fondled.

"You recognize it?" they cried hopefully. "We are glad to restore it to your collection." Almost they started up.

"Hmmmm," I said. They subsided nervously. "The jaw, you see. It doesn't—"

"Doesn't what?" the nephew challenged. "I'm sure it's just like you loaned it to him."

"It's not mine," I said bluntly, "and besides that I'll tell you something. There are two of them—individually represented, I mean. The jaw doesn't fit the skull. It belonged to someone else. You can see by the color it's out of a different grave."

"Two of them," murmured the niece.

"Out of a different grave," repeated the nephew.

I waited patiently. After a time he came to the point. Some see it more rapidly than others.

"I guess Uncle Tobias was—uh—uh—a collector," he said. "We should now like to present his collection to you —or your institution—anonymously, of course."

"Of course," I said. "Would you like a receipt? Would you like to take the box back with you?"

"Thank you, no," said the niece. "You're too kind. And it will be an anonymous gift?"

"We have many of them," I said. "Many of them."

As they went down the steps I saw them walking more lightly. Their arms swung better without the burden. They ran to the car at the curb. On the desk the skull waited. It was a rich old brown, I saw as my hand went over it—a rich old mahogany brown. They needn't have been so jittery—that skull had been hundreds of years underground when Uncle Tobias was born. But where had he got it—and that jaw from another body?

"There's no accounting," I said, "for tastes. Tobias must have been a collector." I said it disapprovingly to the nearest cabinet. Then I picked the skull up and put it inside. I was not, you see, a genuine collector. My motivations were purely scientific and unemotional.

Or were they? I went back to the desk and sat down. I could see Uncle Tobias's long-hidden relic staring back vacantly at me through the glass door of the cabinet. It would never tell its secret, but it had one. It had a secret and so had Uncle Tobias. And I? Perhaps I was a keeper of secrets. Or of orphans, I thought, as my eyes ran along the shelf overhead. And at last I knew where it had begun. Behind the steady chipping of the pick that began to sound in my ears was another sound—the creaking of weathered timbers and the uneasy movement of stormy air in a closed place. That would be it, I thought suddenly—the heads in Hagerty's barn.

II

When Grandma was alone in the kitchen we used to bake heads together in the kitchen stove. When I first approached her on this matter she naturally demurred, but in the end her cooking enthusiasm got the better of her and she would line them up like biscuits in a pie tin and put them in the oven. It was before the days of Charles Addams and we never conceived of ourselves as monsters. It is probably true, however, that it was at this time I developed a mild antipathy for the normal human skull.

This was not my grandmother's fault. In fact, at times, out of some lingering religious scruple she would protest the nature of some of the heads in the oven—opening the door now and then and peering in, partly to see that they were properly done and partly to grumble over their strangeness.

They were clay, burnt clay, and modeled as well as a boy could model skulls he had never handled. Some of them had matchstick teeth or bits of pearl shell from broken buttons. The eyes were the hollow eyes of skulls and the mandibles were shaped as I thought they should be shaped, from drawings in the red-brick museum that I frequented. As for the cranium itself, practically everything I made was slope-browed and primitive. Even today I am apt to be faintly repelled by skulls with no brow ridges or teeth of too delicate a cast.

"Mind you," Grandma would protest, tapping me with a roasting fork, "this is getting out of hand. Them's no ordinary heads in there and no young'un can tell me so. They've got that *look*, they have. That Darwin look. You be staying out of that building now. There's things there wasn't intended to be seen—not by anybody.

"You've got to stop it, youngster," she would say finally and swing the range door shut with a great clang. "You've got to stop it 'fore the Devil gets you by the foot. That little one there looks no more'n half a man. Where'd you find him, boy? Speak out now. Not from any book in this house, I'll warrant."

"No, Grandma, honest not."

"Where then?"

"The room, Grandma, the room in the museum. I climbed up on the railing and looked close. His head was just like that—no forehead—and there was a big card with long words, and there was another head—ordinary— a plain old ordinary head beside him—"

"That's enough, boy, that's enough. They're done now.

Get 'em out of the house. Take 'em away. Out of doors now. And don't touch 'em till they cool."

I never did. When they were cool enough, I put them in a little bag I carried and then I went halfway down the block to Hagerty's barn. It was an old sagging weather-beaten stable, locked up and unused. I knew where a board could be edged aside, however, and there was just room enough to scrape in and let the board drop in place behind me. I always waited then until my eyes were adjusted to the light that came in through cracks and knotholes. In the spring when the light came in through the leaves outside it made a kind of green-lit secrecy.

Then I would take the bag of heads in my teeth and climb by way of some nailed crosspieces way up into the shadows under the roof. There was a half-loft up there—pretty rickety, but it would still bear a boy's weight. I could see after a while, even in that light, and then I would open the bag and take out the heads.

No one but Grandma and I ever saw them. Though I strove in my modelings for painstaking accuracy, it was only because without it the things seemed less real, less alive somehow. They were smaller than life, the size of big marbles, perhaps. Nevertheless they had a peculiar significance to me, a kind of being—the *anima* that exists in all properly shaped miniatures.

Up there under the barn roof I laid them out in little rows along the cross-beams. It was my museum, like the red-brick museum that my grandmother distrusted. Only in my museum nothing was dead. It was filled with a kind of patient, unwinking persistence—the persistence of a half-bewitched league of jack-o'-lantern faces waiting for me to come and sit with them in the green light high in the loft.

In the end I deserted them. There was no help for it. We moved away in what, to my mother, was a small triumph. I had no luggage of my own and no place to conceal the heads.

I can still remember that white, frosty morning and the cold clatter of hoofs as the cab rolled on its way toward the station. Away over the edge of the trees I could see the broken wind vane on Hagerty's stable, pointing steadily, as it always did, in one direction, no wind ever turning it. The heads were there. They would be there till the building fell.

"We will never come back here, son. Never." My mother's voice rang harshly over the cobblestones. But all the time I could feel the magnetic pull of those heads in Hagerty's stable. They would be there in the gray light and the green light; they would be there till the building fell.

III

Fainter than spider silk to my nearsighted gaze, the map lines run under the magnifying glass across a tumbled expanse of southwestern desert and lava beds. Names like Big Hatchet and Buckhorn still bring that vast and ominous landscape into my mind. Though the white man has taken it, it will never be rid of the ghosts of its last owners —the Apaches. It is their bones that lie in the cold on nameless peaks and in the red clay of the washes. Cochise, Victorio, Nana, and Geronimo will haunt it always. In the seventies of the last century many men died here. Dozens of others, the historians say, were never accounted for— the desert swallowed them up. Old Mr. Harney knew; he had been one of the missing. But it was from his family that I first got a hint of his story.

"He keeps her in the china closet," one of them told me, "right with the dishes."

"Kinfolk," sniffed another, with a gesture of distaste.

"The skull of Aunt Lucinda," explained a grandson with less heat. "He never buried her."

"Oh?" I said, puzzled and tactful, while the relatives all chattered together. They would have to make it clear. I had come at their invitation.

"He liked meeting you," they finally got out in chorus. "We think maybe you could influence him."

"Influence?" I said.

"The skull," they countered. "He won't bury it. But he's curious about your work. Maybe you could persuade him to give it to you. He's restless about it. Old, you know, quite old. We don't like having her there. It isn't right. Nor proper. People say—" They tapped their heads in unison like little marionettes.

"It was barbed wire," Mr. Harney said, "it was barbed wire finished our world." He was eighty years old, and the skull lay on the table before us. We sat silent, gazing out into the clear white desert sunlight. Eighty years, I thought, and reached out and turned the skull gently over. Years of smoking pistols and Apaches riding fast through the narrow canyons.

"You have lived a long life," I said. He sighed then, and began talking—the merest wisp of a sound. I leaned forward to catch it.

"Six years in that valley after the haul from Texas, and me a youngster of ten. Mother dead on the trail. Her younger sister, Aunt Lucinda, raised me—the old man meanin' well but ridin'—ridin' most of the time. It took plenty ridin' to hold things together without the wire.

"Sure, we knew there was Apaches in the hills, always was. But people had a way of stickin'. A way—" he paused and reached out as if to touch the nearest blue hill —"as though they liked somethin' here—the air, maybe, so clear, or all this land at sunset, or maybe the feel of it, no fence from Texas to the Big Horns. Or maybe, like me, you had just followed along 'cause your people was moving and they was your people and you didn't go askin' 'em why their names changed along those little roads from the East.

"Lucinda was young and pretty with hair like the sheen on a blackbird's feather, and as good to me as my own mother. Young enough to play and imagine things the way a kid will. When my father was gone she used to play in the yard with me. Aaahh"—the old man got out something between a sigh and a groan—"it didn't last long.

"One night Pa didn't come home. Nobody knows what that means any more. They can't. The miles of darkness creeping in, and a woman and a kid sittin' in a shack waitin' for a man that ain't comin' back no more. You sit there and you dassent light the light for fear of drawin' 'em. And all the time you know they know about you, and it's no good, they'll take their time.

"They got us in the morning, in the first light, with Lucinda standin' out there lookin' for Pa. One of 'em just picked her off out of the mesquite. I'm old, but I've never got it out of my head, so that sometimes I see it like now, with people and things of years later all shadows, and just me with my hand at my mouth, and that shot. She stood there a minute all young and pretty with her hands stretched out to me. And all that love flowed up in her a minute and held her as if she wouldn't fall, and I ran toward her not thinkin' of anything except, as a kid will, that in the circle of such love I must be safe.

"And then she gave a little sigh and that light went out of her and she pitched face down into a clump of prickly pear. They took me then, squalling and kicking, and put me on a horse. After that I was an Apache till I was fifteen."

The faded old eyes turned slowly over the whole compass of the horizon as though they remembered every peak and gully. He didn't offer to go on.

"Mr. Harney," I chided.

"Mexico," he said. "We rode into Old Mexico. They was Victorio's men. And I learned to be an Apache. Kids learn quick. That's why I lived. Ride, shoot, steal. Live on nothing. Trust nobody, and keep ridin'—keep ridin'. South of the border, north of the border, it was all the same.

"Apaches! Y'know, son, that's a joker. We wasn't Apaches. We was a way of life. We lived so hard that half the kids in camp was stolen. Most of 'em Mexicans, stolen south of the border. Raised Apaches. It was the only way to keep our strength up.

"Maybe I was a little old. Maybe I remembered too much. Anyhow I used to see Victorio watching me." Again he paused, searching his memories. "You know, in the end I didn't hate them. I was beginning to look at it the way they did, and to nurse the same feelings. I'd been shot at a lot and seen Indian families and kids I knew disappear. In the end I would have stayed with them, I guess. I spoke the language by then. I could get along." He stopped and whispered to himself a moment in syllables that were not English. Then he went on.

"Victorio must have thought different. Either that or he'd taken a shine to me—I never knew. He was a great warrior and Geronimo was nothing compared to him. He was hard, but there was a kind of bigness in him. When I was fifteen we were sitting on our horses one day looking down into a little town from the hills. I could see people in the streets, and smoke in chimneys. We watched it like animals must watch people—curious and sharp and wild. I watched like everyone else, ready to vanish at the least sign of danger.

"The next thing I knew, Victorio had edged his horse up beside me. 'Those are your people,' he said soft and low and searching my face with his eyes. 'Do you remember?'

"And I looked at him and was afraid, and suddenly the face of Lucinda came to me and I looked back at him, speaking Apache, and I said, 'Yes, I remember.'

"And he nodded, a little sad, and said, 'They are your people. Go down to them.' Then he spoke a word behind me and the thirty people of his band were gone.

" 'I don't know how—' I said. 'My people,' I said, and stopped. It came to me that all the people I had were Apache, and that I was Apache, too.

"Not a muscle of Victorio's face moved. 'Those are your people,' he said, pointing. 'We killed your father and the black-haired one. The white men will take care of you. You are not one of us.' With that he whirled his horse. I never saw him again.

"After a little while I picked my way down and spoke some words of English. It was slow work, like an old hinge squeaking in the wind. People came up to me and stared at my rags and at the pony."

Harney paused, considering, then he said flatly, "It wasn't so uncommon then—changing sides like that. There was room for two lives, and sometimes you had no choice. I got to be a white man even if I was a little late catchin' up. It was really about the same life: ride, shoot, kill. No difference, really, none to amount to anything. Not then, anyhow."

His eyes came almost shut against the midday heat shimmer that was beginning to roil the air out on the flats. I was afraid he was beginning to lose interest and go to sleep. I pushed the skull toward him. "The skull, Mr. Harney," I prodded. "You promised to tell me about the skull. It's a nice thing. Well cared for, too. A woman, I take it. Young. You can tell by the basilar suture. See?"

His eyes opened a little way, defensively, I thought.

"Aahh," he said again in that voice I was beginning to learn meant something hurt him. "It was afterward, sometime, that the thought came to me. I rode back to the old place. Nobody had been there all those years. And I found her—a few little bits of white bone, that is, and the skull in a drift of sand with the prickly pear grown over it. The hair," and with this he put up a careful, stroking finger, "was all gone. You wouldn't think it would go away so fast. For a while I looked around.

"Then it came on me I should bury her—and she out in the heat and dust and among bone-cracking coyotes so long. But what was there to bury, really? And besides this is a big wide land where you see miles as long as you can see at all. Every day of your life you see that way. And it's hard to be underground afterward. I had lived on the land enough to know.

"In the end I knew I couldn't bury her there. She was the only kin I had, so I took her up carefully and rode back with her. I figured at first maybe I'd have it done in a proper ceremony with a churchyard and a preacher to ease it a little.

"But then I couldn't. I couldn't face up to it. I kept putting it off and getting that feeling that if I did bury her she would go away; that she wouldn't be real any longer. I settled on this place finally and I kept Lucinda safe in the china closet. She never had to be afraid any more, and she could look out through the glass. Sometimes I talked to her.

"I'm a grown man, but that I did not get over, do you see—though I know all's dark in the grave and this is cold bone on the table top. I have a wife and sons, but this I will not bear—that they should put her under the ground with me."

He reached out and clutched my wrist and I cursed my easy juggling with anatomy a moment before. One of the family made a sign to me from the doorway.

I stood up then and took his hand and said quickly, by way of comfort, "She will not want to look through the glass at strange faces. Let her go with you. One can stay too long in the sun."

"Aahh," he said blindly, and took her back into his

hands, fumbling. "It's plain you are not one of the open people, or you would not say that. It's the wire," he said, his voice subsiding once more to a thin whisper that seemed to come out of the grass beside us. "It's the wire that's made a difference. No wire from Texas to the Big Horns. It was all space and bright sun."

A granddaughter led him away.

IV

I wouldn't have taken old Mr. Harney's skull, even if he had offered it to me, for anything in the world. He had assumed a personal responsibility there that was not transferable. I knew too much of the story, and yet I was not part of it. Young Aunt Lucinda would have haunted me. Not physically, perhaps, but with that kind of intangible loneliness that comes of knowing about events behind you in time that you can never alter or intrude within, and yet there is somebody there you know or love, or wish greatly to have comforted, but it is back behind you and of all things the loneliest. So I left Harney with that burden as all men are left with it. It was his time, and he would have to deal with it as best he could.

Now, years later, I have some intimation of the emotions that had shaken him. I get out all the skulls. A massive unknown cranium which bears the look of the Cro-Magnon past about it is one I rescued from a medical dissecting room. I touch with fondness a mineralized skull vault whose age I can never prove but that rolled, I well know, for ages in the glacial gravels of the Platte. I look at them all, these silent masks whose teeth I have mended and whose mortal rags I have patched together with preservatives. Where will they go after the years of comfort— these fading, anonymous individuals who have somehow come to have a claim upon me? Scientifically they are worthless, for museums scrutinize with ever greater care the credentials of the bones that are donated to their skull rooms.

What chance has a dissecting room specimen without a pedigree? Should I hide him as Tobias did, in the attic, and hope for a kinder time? Should I seek to protect him by surreptitiously introducing him into a cemetery vault? Well, you see the problem.

And it is a burden, too. I realize it more as I get older, and I know, now, why Tobias the lawyer left that unrecorded legacy in his attic. What else could he do? Most people don't look at these things in the same way, and it's just as well they don't. Otherwise we would be like certain Indian tribes who had to move the cemetery with them when they migrated. The attitude is easier to catch than you think. I know two men who have moved dead wives.

Generally I can't refuse skulls that are offered to me. It is not that I am morbid, or a true collector, or that I need many of them in my work. It is just that in most cases, people being what they are, I know the skulls are safer with me. Call it a kind of respect for the bones, ingrained through long habit. That, I guess, is the reason I keep those two locked in the filing cabinet—they are delicate, and not in a position to defend themselves. So I look out for them. I'd do as much for you.

8

THE RELIC MEN

I

So the reporters follow you into that place without roads and they say: "Give us the story, Doctor. Give us the dope." Overhead a turkey vulture spirals slowly out of sight on an updraft of air.

You look everywhere—at your shoes and the poised, eager pencils—and you say, clearing your throat a little, "A remarkable discovery, gentlemen. These remains constitute a new species from the terminal Pleistocene fauna. The bones are associated with human artifacts. Such excellent preservation is rare. It is our belief—"

"No, no, Doctor," they protest. "Give us some human interest. Never mind that Pleistocene business. Tell us how many years. And they're broken. How did they get broken? Maybe there was a fight, huh?"

"Human interest, why, uh, yes, human interest," you counter, thinking in the back of your mind, "Look, I'm human, too, and this is my interest." But that doesn't count, you know that. Haven't there been these articles, "We Can't Hear You, Professor"? Brace up, now, this is the press.

"What's the angle, Professor? Who found it?"

You try once more. "The site has been excavated by the State University, which I represent. The site was called to our attention by—" A warm feeling suffuses you. You point. A shabby little man with a tobacco-stained mustache stands at the edge of the trench, peering in. He looks pleased and wondering. "Mr. Johnson, there, he found it. He's been looking for years—"

"Okay, Professor. And you came all the way out here for this thing? Must have been important, all right. How are you going to put it all back together? You fellows always do that from a single bone, don't you?"

"No, we don't. It depends," you protest wearily, but the man isn't listening. His pencil is busy. Then he turns and taps you with it.

"We might take your picture with that bone, Doctor. It's about the only way to get any human interest into a science like this. We've got to show people what it's all about. If they don't see it, they're not interested. I'll send Ed over for the camera."

The car makes a little splash of sound in the wide prairie silence. The silence flows back minute by minute, the High Plains silence that has swallowed a quarter of your lifetime. You sigh, and your knees feel unaccountably weak. You sit on the edge of the trench and press your hands into the warm soil. The thing is out of your hands now. That reporter—a nice young fellow—knows what he's after. Odd what people are interested in and what they make of it. I remember—

II

I remember the sound of the wind in that country never stopped. I think everyone there was a little mad because of it. In the end I suppose I was like all the rest. It was a country of topsyturvy, where great dunes of sand blew slowly over ranch houses and swallowed them, and where, after the sand had all blown away from under your feet, the beautiful arrowheads of ice-age hunters lay mingled with old whisky bottles that the sun had worked upon. I suppose, now that I stop to think about it, that if there is any place in the world where a man might fall in love with a petrified woman, that may be the place.

In the proper books, you understand, there is no such thing as a petrified woman, and I insist that when I first came to that place I would have said the same. It all happened because bone hunters are listeners. They have to be.

We had had terrible luck that season. We had made queries in a score of towns and tramped as many canyons. The institution for which we worked had received a total of one Oligocene turtle and a bag of rhinoceros bones. A rag picker could have done better. The luck had to change. Somewhere there had to be fossils.

I was cogitating on the problem under a coating of lather in a barbershop with an 1890 chair when I became aware of a voice. You can hear a lot of odd conversation in barbershops, particularly in the back country, and particularly if your trade makes you a listener, as mine does. But what caught my ear at first was something about stone. Stone and bone are pretty close in my language and I wasn't missing any bets. There was always a chance that there might be a bone in it somewhere for me.

The voice went off into a grumbling rural complaint in the back corner of the shop, and then it rose higher.

"It's petrified! It's petrified!" the voice contended excitedly.

I managed to push an ear up through the lather.

"I'm a-tellin' ya," the man boomed, "a petrified woman, right out in that canyon. But he won't show it, not to nobody. 'Tain't fair, I tell ya."

"Mister," I said, speaking warily between the barber's razor and his thumb, "I'm reckoned a kind of specialist in these matters. Where is this woman, and how do you know she's petrified?"

I knew perfectly well she wasn't, of course. Flesh doesn't petrify like wood or bone, but there are plenty of people who think it does. In the course of my life I've been offered objects that ranged from petrified butterflies to a gentleman's top hat.

Just the same, I was still interested in this woman. You can never tell what will turn up in the back country. Once I had a mammoth vertebra handed to me with the explanation that it was a petrified griddle cake. Mentally, now, I was trying to shape that woman's figure into the likeness of a mastodon's femur. This is a hard thing to do when you are young and far from the cities. Nevertheless, I managed it. I held that shining bony vision in my head and asked directions of my friend in the barbershop.

Yes, he told me, the woman was petrified all right. Old man Buzby wasn't a feller to say it if it 'tweren't so. And it weren't no part of a woman. It was a *whole* woman. Buzby had said that, too. But Buzby was a queer one. An old bachelor, you know. And when the boys had wanted to see it, 'count of it bein' a sort of marvel around these parts, the old man had clammed up on where it was. A-keepin' it all to hisself, he was. But seein' as I was interested in these things and a stranger, he might talk to me and no harm done. It was the trail to the right and out and up to the overhang of the hills. A little tarpapered shack there.

I asked Mack to go up there with me. He was silent company but one of the best bone hunters we had. Whether it was a rodent the size of a bee or an elephant the size of a house, he'd find it and he'd get it out, even if it meant that we carried a five-hundred-pound plaster cast on foot over a mountain range.

In a day we reached the place. When I got out of the car I knew the wind had been blowing there since time began. There was a rusty pump in the yard and rusty wire and rusty machines nestled in the lee of a wind-carved butte. Everything was leaching and blowing away by degrees, even the tarpaper on the roof.

Out of the door came Buzby. He was not blowing away, I thought at first. His farm might be, but he wasn't. There was an air of faded dignity about him.

Now in that country there is a sort of etiquette. You don't drive out to a man's place, a bachelor's, and you a stranger, and come up to his door and say: "I heard in town you got a petrified woman here, and brother, I sure would like to see it." You've got to use tact, same as anywhere else.

You get out slowly while the starved hounds look you over and get their barking done. You fumble for your pipe and explain casually you're doin' a little lookin' around in the hills. About that time they get a glimpse of the equipment you're carrying and most of them jump to the conclusion that you're scouting for oil. You can see the hope flame up in their eyes and sink down again as you explain you're just hunting bones. Some of them don't believe you after that. It's a hard thing to murder a poor man's dream.

But Buzby wasn't the type. I don't think he even thought of the oil. He was small and neat and wore—I swear it—pince-nez glasses. I could see at a glance that he was a city man dropped, like a seed, by the wind. He had been there a long time, certainly. He knew the corn talk and the heat talk, but he would never learn how to come forward in that secure, heavy-shouldered country way, to lean on a car door and talk to strangers while the horizon stayed in his eyes.

He invited us, instead, to see his collection of arrowheads. It looked like a good start. We dusted ourselves and followed him in. It was a two-room shack, and about as comfortable as a monk's cell. It was neat, though, so neat you knew that the man lived, rather than slept there. It lacked the hound-asleep-in-the-bunk confusion of the usual back-country bachelor's quarters.

He was precise about his Indian relics as he was precise about everything, but I sensed after a while a touch of pathos—the pathos of a man clinging to order in a world where the wind changed the landscape before morning, and not even a dog could help you contain the loneliness of your days.

"Someone told me in town you might have a wonderful fossil up here," I finally ventured, poking in his box of arrowheads, and watching the shy, tense face behind the glasses.

"That would be Ned Burner," he said. "He talks too much."

"I'd like to see it," I said, carefully avoiding the word *woman*. "It might be something of great value to science."

He flushed angrily. In the pause I could hear the wind beating at the tarpaper.

"I don't want any of 'em hereabouts to see it," he cried passionately. "They'll laugh and they'll break it and it'll be gone like—like everything." He stopped, uncertainly aware of his own violence, his dark eyes widening with pain.

"We are scientists, Mr. Buzby," I urged gently. "We're not here to break anything. We don't have to tell Ned Burner what we see."

He seemed a little mollified at this, then a doubt struck

him. "But you'd want to take her away, put her in a museum."

I noticed the pronoun but ignored it. "Mr. Buzby," I said, "we would very much like to see your discovery. It may be we can tell you more about it that you'd like to know. It might be that a museum would help you save it from vandals. I'll leave it to you. If you say no, we won't touch it, and we won't talk about it in the town, either. That's fair enough, isn't it?"

I could see him hesitating. It was plain that he wanted to show us, but the prospect was half-frightening. Oddly enough, I had the feeling his fright revolved around his discovery, more than fear of the townspeople. As he talked on, I began to see what he wanted. He intended to show it to us in the hope we would confirm his belief that it was a petrified woman. The whole thing seemed to have taken on a tremendous importance in his mind. At that point, I couldn't fathom his reasons.

Anyhow, he had something. At the back of the house we found the skull of a big, long-horned, extinct bison hung up under the eaves. It was a nice find, and we coveted it.

"It needs a dose of alvar for preservation," I said. "The museum would be the place for a fine specimen like this. It will just go slowly to pieces here."

Buzby was not unattentive. "Maybe, Doctor, maybe. But I have to think. Why don't you camp here tonight? In the morning—"

"Yes?" I said, trying to keep the eagerness out of my voice. "You think we might—?"

"No! Well, yes, all right. But the conditions? They're like you said?"

"Certainly," I answered. "It's very kind of you."

He hardly heard me. That glaze of pain passed over his face once more. He turned and went into the house without speaking. We did not see him again until morning.

The wind goes down into those canyons also. It starts on the flats and rises through them with weird noises, flaking and blasting at every loose stone or leaning pinnacle. It scrapes the sand away from pipy concretions till they stand out like strange distorted sculptures. It leaves great stones teetering on wineglass stems.

I began to suspect what we would find, the moment I came there. Buzby hurried on ahead now, eager and panting. Once he had given his consent and started, he seemed in almost a frenzy of haste.

Well, it was the usual thing. Up. Down. Up. Over boulders and splintered deadfalls of timber. Higher and higher into the back country. Toward the last he outran us, and I couldn't hear what he was saying. The wind whipped it away.

But there he stood, finally, at a niche under the canyon wall. He had his hat off and, for a moment, was oblivious to us. He might almost have been praying. Anyhow I stood back and waited for Mack to catch up. "This must be it," I said to him. "Watch yourself." Then we stepped forward.

It was a concretion, of course—an oddly shaped lump of mineral matter—just as I had figured after seeing the wind at work in those miles of canyon. It wasn't a bad job, at that. There were some bumps in the right places, and a few marks that might be the face, if your imagination was strong. Mine wasn't just then. I had spent a day building a petrified woman into a mastodon femur, and now that was no good either, so I just stood and looked.

But after the first glance it was Buzby I watched. The unskilled eye can build marvels of form where the educated see nothing. I thought of that bison skull under his eaves, and how badly we needed it.

He didn't wait for me to speak. He blurted with a terrible intensity that embarrassed me, "She—she's beautiful, isn't she?"

"It's remarkable," I said. "Quite remarkable." And then I just stood there not knowing what to do.

He seized on my words with such painful hope that Mack backed off and started looking for fossils in places where he knew perfectly well there weren't any.

I didn't catch it all; I couldn't possibly. The words came out in a long, aching torrent, the torrent dammed up for years in the heart of a man not meant for this place, nor for the wind at night by the windows, nor the empty bed, nor the neighbors twenty miles away. You're tough at first. He must have been to stick there. And then suddenly you're old. You're old and you're beaten, and there must be something to talk to and to love. And if you haven't got it you'll make it in your head, or out of a stone in a canyon wall.

He had found her, and he had a myth of how she came there, and now he came up and talked to her in the long afternoon heat while the dust devils danced in his failing corn. It was progressive. I saw the symptoms. In another year, she would be talking to him.

"It's true, isn't it, Doctor?" he asked me, looking up with that rapt face, after kneeling beside the niche. "You can see it's her. You can see it plain as day." For the life of me I couldn't see anything except a red scar writhing on the brain of a living man who must have loved somebody once, beyond words and reason.

"Now Mr. Buzby," I started to say then, and Mack came up and looked at me. This, in general, is when you launch into a careful explanation of how concretions are made so that the layman will not make the same mistake again. Mack just stood there looking at me in that stolid way of his. I couldn't go on with it. I couldn't even say it.

But I saw where this was going to end. I saw it suddenly and too late. I opened my mouth while Mr. Buzby clasped his hands and tried to regain his composure. I opened my mouth and I lied in a way to damn me forever in the halls of science.

I lied, looking across at Mack, and I could feel myself getting redder every moment. It was a stupendous, a colossal lie. "Mr. Buzby," I said, "that—um—er—figure is astonishing. It is a remarkable case of preservation. We must have it for the museum."

The light in his face was beautiful. He believed me now. He believed himself. He came up to the niche again, and touched her lovingly.

"It's okay," I whispered to Mack. "We won't have to pack the thing out. He'll never give her up."

That's where I was a fool. He came up to me, his eyes troubled and unsure, but very patient.

"I think you're right, Doctor," he said. "It's selfish of me. She'll be safer with you. If she stays here somebody will smash her. I'm not well." He sat down on a rock and wiped his forehead. "I'm sure I'm not well. I'm sure she'll be safer with you. Only I don't want her in a glass case where people can stare at her. If you can promise that, I—"

"I can promise that," I said, meeting Mack's eyes across Buzby's shoulder.

"And if I come there I can see her?"

I knew I would never meet him again in this life.

"Yes," I said, "you can see her there." I waited, and then I said, "We'll get the picks and plaster ready. Now that bison skull at your house . . ."

It was two days later, in the truck, that Mack spoke to me. "Doc."

"Yeah."

"You know what the Old Man is going to say about shipping that concretion. It's heavy. Must be three hundred pounds with the plaster."

"Yes, I know."

Mack was pulling up slow along the abutment of a

bridge. It was the canyon of the big Piney, a hundred miles away. He got out and went to the rear of the truck. I didn't say anything, but I followed him back.

"Doc, give me a hand with this, will you?"

I took one end, and we heaved together. It's a long drop in the big Piney. I didn't look, but I heard it break on the stones.

"I wish I hadn't done that," I said.

"It was only a concretion," Mack answered. "The old geezer won't know."

"I don't like it," I said. "Another week in that wind and I'd have believed in her myself. Get me the hell out of here—maybe I do, anyhow. I tell you I don't like it. I don't like it at all."

"It's a hundred more to Valentine," Mack said.

He put the map in the car pocket and slid over and gave me the wheel.

III

The devil, in the eyes of many devout Fundamentalists, occupies the bone lands, the waste places at the margins of everyday existence. I never knew but one who thought differently and who considered that God, too, might have something to do with the edges of the known.

Most men proceed under a burden of fear, and the majority of them in my youth could not stand the sight of a bone hunter. He was associated in their minds with the search for the missing link. At the very least he was apt to appear triumphantly waving the thigh bone of some creature not mentioned in Holy Writ. His ways were queer ways, and he suffered for them. At best he was regarded with tolerant amusement; at the worst, he would have screen doors latched against him.

It was that way in the Valley of the Pumpkin Seed. To

compound our misery, we learned at the local newspaper office that the only impressive bone in the whole county—a veritable giant of a bone—was owned by a devout member of a sect which lent no ear to modern geological heresies. This word was carried on lagging and pessimistic feet to the Director.

"Well," he said, kicking dubiously at a loose rock in the roadway, "there's nothing to do but try. He must have found it somewhere around here. What do you suppose he saved it for—a chap like that? Most of them would have broken it up for lime fertilizer. Something curious there. Let's go and ask him. I'll go myself."

There was a road up through the outliers of the Wildcat hills, and by and by, a gate. We descended self-consciously while a horde of screeching children broke and ran for the house. It was a soddy. Forty years ago you could still see them sometimes on the Pumpkin Seed.

First there was the woman with the children peering from behind her skirts. She didn't latch the door, but she stood there with about the same stance that I remember my grandmother used to assume when she described the time she chased some Pawnee out of the hayfield.

We stopped at a respectful distance. "Good morning, ma'am," we said. "Would the Mister be about now? We would like to see that fossil bone he's got. The one people think is an elephant's bone. We heard about it in town. We're from the University."

The woman's expression did not change. There was silence for a moment, while we fingered our hats uneasily. Then she lifted her voice. "Pa," she called uncertainly. "There's some men in the yard. Relic men, I reckon."

Mr. Mullens' moustache was straw yellow, and it contrasted oddly with his face, which was blue-tinged because of an aggravated heart condition. The moment I saw him I felt a great sense of relief. He had the merry, wondering, wandering eye of the born naturalist. Poor, uneducated, reared in a sect which frowns upon natural science, some wind out of the Pliocene had touched him. He threw wide the door and made a great, sweeping gesture that propelled us almost bodily into the room.

"Boys," he chuckled, "I been a-waitin' for ye. I knew ye'd come to see the bone. Didn't I tell ye, Carrie? Didn't I tell ye they'd be here?" Carrie, her fortress taken, retired with a weary air into the kitchen.

"Now boys," said Mr. Mullens, "we'll git to business. That bone ain't all, not by a jugful. There's more where that come from." He breathed heavily with the excitement of the moment. His lips turned a little more blue.

"There it is, boys." He swept the parlor curtain aside. A great brown bone, seamed with the weather onslaughts of more than a million years, stood upright on a pedestal behind the curtain.

"My god," said the Director, "there's no mistaking that —it's elephant." He used the term generically, as the bone men always do, to cover a score of species of vanished mammoth and mastodon.

"That's what I told 'em," said Mr. Mullens proudly. "I told 'em it were too big for a cow, or a horse or anythin' in these parts. It's an elyphant."

His breathing began to labor like something whispering apart from him. "I found it in the hills out there, just twenty years ago. I fixed it, too, brought it home and poured glue in her to harden. Been keepin' her ever since."

"Twenty years," murmured the Director dejectedly. I knew what was in his mind. "Look, Mr. Mullens, do you think you can remember how to get there?"

"Can I remember how to get there?" said Mr. Mullens with proper contempt for our lack of faith. "Listen to the man. I been over these hills for fifty years! I'll take ye there myself."

The breathing began to whisper behind his words again. "I tell you this ain't all. I saw bones all over that valley, scattered up and down a-shinin' in the sun. I tell ye," he paused to gather strength for his intellectual effort, "I got a notion about it.

"I figure it's a place where all the garbage from the Flood—them big animals and pore human sinners—all got carried along and dropped when the water went back where it came from. The sinners and the elyphants all a-tossin' and a-rollin' and a-grindin' together till the good Lord saw fit to lay 'em down.

"It's the garbage from the biggest Flood of all, lads— come right down to our valley. And that there thigh bone I picked up off the hillside. The marvel of it struck me. I was scared green, but I wanted it. I wanted to bring it home. I ain't never been back and I ain't never told nobody. But it's all there, boys—I know it's there, an' I'll show ye. I'm not what you'd call spry, but I'll show ye. I got a hankerin'—a hankerin' to see it once more—that hill and that valley and them big bones all a-shinin' in the sun."

I don't know whether anybody said "Amen," but I knew what we were all thinking: Could the old man deliver? Ninety-nine out of every hundred of these stories is spun out of thin air. It is the hundredth chance that the bone hunter plays for. That means, really, that he cannot afford to neglect anybody's story; the worst of them may contain a germ of truth or, at the very least, a bone. But a quarry is the thing, a real fossil quarry. They don't come easy. There are only a few in the world.

It was in this frame of mind that we started with Dad Mullens. We were warmed by his unexpected friendliness, but as for his tall tale, that was another matter entirely. I didn't believe a word of it, and I knew that the Director, as befitted a seasoned veteran, believed even less. All we hoped was that the old boy might just possibly remember and be able to guide us to the spot where he had found that huge thigh bone. The big, brown femur, the color of oakwood, was real enough, whatever else may have ballooned out of Mr. Mullens's obviously powerful gift for words.

We drove across sand banks and up dry arroyos; we rose and fell over short grass prairie. We lowered fence wire and intruded on the privacy of range cattle so remote from civilization that they never went to market. We came at last to a barrier of stony hills.

"What do we do now, Dad?" someone asked. The old man stood upright beside me. He peered at those hills like a Spaniard pursuing the seven golden cities. "It's somewhere hereabouts," he called to us. "But I jist can't seem to recollect quite where. I think we'd better press on a piece back into the hills. Just leave the cars here, boys. They won't go no further."

There were five hills, there were ten hills, and at the last it may have been twenty-five. We scaled them all, you see. Our Stout Cortez had to look for an appropriate point, a commanding view. I tell you he scared the daylights out of me. He wheezed and choked and he turned bluer and blacker, but he kept picking bigger hills to climb.

"Dad," I croaked, "for the love of God, you're killing yourself. We can't go on like this. You've just forgotten in twenty years, that's all. There's nothing to be ashamed of. Let's just go back now and forget it. We believe you, all right. We know you saw it. But maybe the good Lord didn't aim for you to see it again."

"Hallelujah!" the old man bellowed, ignoring me. "This is the place."

There was a late afternoon sun playing on that hillside, and I can remember still the way my eyes traveled down it from boulder to gray boulder between the spines of Spanish bayonet. And then I saw it. Maybe this won't mean anything to you. Maybe you don't understand this game, or why men follow it. But I saw it. I tell you I saw five million years of the planet's history lying there on that hillside with the yucca growing over it and the roots working through it, just the way the old man had remembered it from a day long ago in the sun.

I saw the ivory from the tusks of elephants scattered like broken china that the rain has washed. I saw the splintered, mineralized enamel of huge unknown teeth. I paused over the bones of ferocious bear-dog carnivores. I saw, protruding from an eroding gully, the jaw of a shovel-tusked amebelodont that has been gone twice a million years into the night of geologic time. I tell you I saw it with my own eyes and I knew, even as I looked at it, that I would never see anything like it again.

The old man stood there muttering about the Flood and seeing, no doubt, his own fearful visions. And while he breathed and whispered, and we waited for the others to explore, I wandered aimlessly as a daisy picker along the hillsides. I touched and picked up and dropped again. I stuffed my pockets and cleaned them out in indecision. We were rich at last—as the bone hunter reckons riches.

The fragments on that weathered hillside were only a hint of the undisturbed treasures that lay in those slowly eroding strata. The place must have represented the shallows of some great Pliocene lake. Into it, over millennia, had washed the bones of hunter and hunted, themselves drifting in the vaster eddies of time. The sabretooth cats had paced there. In the shallows, the shovel-tuskers had scooped and crunched strange water lilies. Now the desert hills lay over their watery kingdom. The bark of the bone hunters' dynamite would disturb their sleep.

A couple of years later we again drove up the path to the old man's soddy. The kids were still there by the gate —a little bigger, but not much. They recognized us and turned and broke for the house.

"Ma," I heard them yell, "Ma, Ma, the relic men are here again!" This time they screeched in expectant enthusiasm.

The old man was not at the door to greet us. The great brown bone still stood on its pedestal in the parlor, but its discoverer was gone. I looked at Carrie mutely. She shook her head. I touched the massive relic. Its owner was safe with Noah now, beyond the waters of the greatest flood of all.

As I went down the hill in the gathering darkness, I shivered. Old Mullens had lived in a small, tight world of marvels, and they had lasted him till the end. Never by word or deed had we intruded upon his beliefs.

A great river of stars spilled southward over the low hills, and a cold wind began to race me onward. Bone hunters were lonely people, I thought briefly, as I turned on the car heat for comfort. It had something to do with time. Perhaps, in the end, we did not know where we belonged.

Perhaps . . . Take that young reporter, for instance; he knew where he belonged, and what to do with human interest. He was tapping me again with his pencil. "All right, Doctor, we're all set. Ed's come back with the camera."

"Never mind the big words, never mind the names of little people. Stand right there and point. It's the best sort of human interest, you and that bone. Just keep pointing. That's it—keep pointing, and we'll have something. Good-by now. Good-by."

9

STRANGENESS IN THE PROPORTION

"**I** MAY truly say," wrote Sir Francis Bacon, in the time of his tragic fall in 1621, "my soul hath been a stranger in the course of my pilgrimage. I seem to have my conversation among the ancients more than among those with whom I live." I suppose, in essence, this is the story of every man who thinks, though there are centuries when such thought grows painfully intense, as in our own. Bacon's contemporary, Shakespeare, also speaks of it from the shadows when he says:

> "Sir, in my heart there was a kinde of fighting,
>   That would not let me sleepe."

In one of those strange, elusive stories upon which Walter de la Mare exerted all the powers of his marvelous poetic gift, a traveler musing over the quaint epitaphs in a country cemetery suddenly grows aware of the cold on a bleak hillside, of the onset of a winter evening, of the miles he has yet to travel, of the solitude he faces. He turns to go and is suddenly confronted by a man who has appeared from no place our traveler can discover, and who has about him, though he is clothed in human garb and form, an unearthly air of difference. The stranger, who appears to be holding a forked twig like that which diviners use, asks of our traveler, the road. "Which," he queries, "is the way?"

The mundane, though sensitive, traveler indicates the high road to town. The stranger, with a look of revulsion upon his face, almost as though it flowed from some secret information transmitted by the forked twig he clutches, recoils in horror. The way—the human way—that the traveler indicates to him is obviously not his way. The stranger has wandered, perhaps like Bacon, out of some more celestial pathway.

When the traveler turns from giving directions, the stranger has gone, not necessarily supernaturally, for de la Mare is careful to move within the realm of the possible, but in a manner that leaves us suddenly tormented with the notion that our road, the road to town, the road of everyday life, has been rejected by a person of divinatory powers who sees in it some disaster not anticipated by ourselves. Suddenly in this magical and evocative winter landscape, the reader asks himself with an equal start of terror, "What *is* the way?" The road we have taken for granted is now filled with the shadowy menace and the anguished revulsion of that supernatural being who exists in all of us. A weird country tale—a ghost story if you will —has made us tremble before our human destiny.

Unlike the creatures who move within visible nature and are indeed shaped by that nature, man resembles the changeling of medieval fairy tales. He has suffered an exchange in the safe cradle of nature, for his earlier instinctive self. He is now susceptible, in the words of theologians, to unnatural desires. Equally, in the view of the evolutionist, he is subject to indefinite departure, but his destination is written in no decipherable tongue.

For in man, by contrast with the animal, two streams of evolution have met and merged: the biological and the cultural. The two streams are not always mutually compatible. Sometimes they break tumultuously against each other so that, to a degree not experienced by any other creature, man is dragged hither and thither, at one moment by the blind instincts of the forest, at the next by the strange intuitions of a higher self whose rationale he doubts and does not understand. He is capable of murder without conscience. He has denied himself thrice over, and is as familiar as Judas with the thirty pieces of silver.

He has come part way into an intangible realm determined by his own dreams. Even the dreams he doubts because they are not fanged and clawed like the life he sees about him. He is tormented, and torments. He loves, and sees his love cruelly rejected by his fellows. Far more than the double evolutionary creatures seen floundering on makeshift flippers from one medium to another, man is marred, transitory, and imperfect.

Man's isolation is even more terrifying if he looks about at his fellow creatures and searches for signs of intelligence behind the universe. As Francis Bacon saw, "all things . . . are full of panic terrors; human things most of all; so infinitely tossed and troubled as they are with superstition (which is in truth nothing but a panic terror) especially in seasons of hardship, anxiety, and adversity."

Unaided, science has little power over human destiny save in a purely exterior and mechanical way. The beacon light of truth, as Hawthorne somewhere remarks, is often surrounded by the flapping wings of ungainly night birds drawn as unerringly as moths toward candlelight. Man's predicament is augmented by the fact that he is alone in the universe. He is locked in a single peculiar body; he can compare observations with no other form of life.

He knows that every step he takes can lead him into some unexplored region from which he may never return. Each individual among us, haunted by memory, reveals this sense of fear. We cling to old photographs and letters because they comfort our intangible need for location in time. For this need of our nature science offers cold comfort. To recognize this, however, is not to belittle the role of science in our world. In his enthusiasm for a new magic, modern man has gone far in assigning to science—his own intellectual invention—a role of omnipotence not inherent in the invention itself. Bacon envisioned science as a powerful and enlightened servant—but never the master—of man.

One of the things which must ever be remembered about Francis Bacon and the depth of his prophetic insight is that it remains, by the nature of his time, in a sense paradoxical. Bacon was one of the first time-conscious moderns. He felt on his brow as did no other man—even men more skilled in the devising of experiment—the wind of the oncoming future, those far-off airs blowing, as he put it in the language of the voyagers, "from the new continent." Ironically, neither king, lawyer, nor scientist could tolerate Bacon's vision of the oncoming future. Because William Harvey was a scientist whose reputation has grown with the years, he is sometimes quoted by scholars even today as demonstrating that Bacon was a literary man who need not be taken seriously by historians of science.

That Bacon was a writer of great powers no one who has read his work would deny. He exercised, in fact, a profound stylistic influence both upon English writers who followed him and upon the scientists of the Royal Society. To say, for this reason, that he is of no scientific significance is to miss his importance as a statesman and philosopher of science as well as to deny to the scientist himself any greater role in discovery than the casual assemblage of facts. Harvey's attitude serves only to illustrate that great experimental scientists are not necessarily equally great philosophers, and that there may be realms denied to them. Similar able but particulate scientists, it could easily be pointed out, wrote disparagingly of Darwin in his time.

The great synthesizer who alters the outlook of a generation, who suddenly produces a kaleidoscopic change in our vision of the world, is apt to be the most envied, feared, and hated man among his contemporaries. Almost by instinct they feel in him the seed of a new order; they sense, even as they anathematize him, the passing away of the sane, substantial world they have long inhabited. Such a man is a kind of lens or gathering point through which past thought gathers, is reorganized, and radiates outward again into new forms.

"There are . . . minds," Emerson once remarked, "that deposit their dangerous unripe thoughts here and there to lie still for a time and be brooded in other minds, and the shell not to be broken until the next age, for them to begin, as new individuals, their career." Francis Bacon was such a man, and it is perhaps for this very reason that there has been visited upon him, by both moralist and scientist alike, so much misplaced vituperation and rejection.

He has been criticized, almost in the same breath, as being falsely termed a scientist and on the other hand as being responsible for all the technological evils from which we suffer in the modern age. His vision was, to a degree, paradoxical. The reason lies in the fact that even the great visionary thinker never completely escapes his own age or the limitations it imposes upon him. Thus Bacon, the weather-tester who held up a finger to the winds of time, was trapped in an age still essentially almost static in its ideas of human duration and in the age and size of man's universe.

A man of the Renaissance, Bacon, for all his cynicism

and knowledge of human frailty, still believed in man. He argues well and lucidly that to begin with doubt is, scientifically, to end in certainty, while to begin in certainty is to end in doubt. He failed to see that science, the doubter, might end in metaphysical doubt itself—doubt of the rationality of the universe, doubt as to the improvability of man. Today the "great machine" that Bacon so well visualized, rolls on, uncontrolled and infinitely devastating, shaking the lives of people in the remote jungles of the Congo as it torments equally the hearts of civilized men.

It is evident from his *New Atlantis* (1624), the Utopian fragment begun toward the end of his life and left unfinished, that this attempt to picture for humanity the state it might attain under science and just rule retains a certain static quality. Bacon is sure about the scientific achievements of his ideal state, but, after all, his pictured paradise is an island without population problems, though medicine there is apparently a high art. Moreover, like most of the Utopias of this period, it is hidden away from the corrupting influence of the world. It is an ideal and moving presentation of men going about their affairs under noble and uplifting circumstances. It is, as someone has remarked, "ourselves made perfect."

But as to how this perfection is to come into being, Bacon is obscure. It is obvious that the wise men of *The New Atlantis* must keep their people from the debasing examples of human behavior in the world outside. Bacon, in other words, has found it easier to picture the growth of what he has termed "experiments of fruit" than to establish the reality of a breed of men worthy to enjoy them. Even the New Atlantis has had to remain armed and hidden, like Elizabethan England behind its sea fogs.

The New Atlantis cannot be read for solutions to the endless permutations and combinations of cultural change, the opened doorway through which Bacon and his followers have thrust us, and through which there is no return.

To Bacon all possible forms of knowledge of the world might be accumulated in a few scant generations. With education the clouded mirror of the mind might be cleansed. "It is true," he admitted in an earlier work, *Valerius Terminus*, "that there is a limitation rather potential than actual which is when the effect is possible, but the time or place yieldeth not matter or basis whereupon man should work."

In this statement we see the modern side of Bacon's mind estimating the play of chance and time. We see it again a few pages later when, in dealing with the logical aspects of contingency, he writes, "our purpose is not to stir up men's hopes but to guide their travels." "Liberty," he continues, speaking in a scientific sense, "is when the direction is not restrained to some definite means, but comprehendeth all the means and ways possible." For want of a variety of scientific choice, he is attempting to say, you may be prevented from achieving a scientific good, some desirable direction down which humanity might travel. The bewildering multiplicity of such roads, the recalcitrance of even educated choice, are not solely to be blamed on Bacon's four-hundred-year gap in experience. In fact, it could readily be contended that science, as he intended to practice it, has not been practiced at all.

Although he has been hailed with some justice as the prophet of industrial science, it is often forgotten that he wished from the beginning to press forward on all scientific fronts at once, instead of pursuing the piecemeal emergence of the various disciplines in the fashion in which investigation was actually carried out. Three centuries have been consumed in establishing certain anthropological facts that he asserted from the beginning. He distinguished cultural and environmental influences completely from the racial factors with which they have been confused down to this day. He advocated the careful study and emulation of the heights of human achievement.

Today scientific studies of "creativity" and the conditions governing the release of such energies in the human psyche are just beginning to be made. He believed and emphasized that it was within man's latent power to draw out of nature, as he puts it, "a second world."

It is here, however, that we come back upon that place of numerous crossroads where man has lifted the lantern of his intellect hopefully to many ambiguous if not treacherous sign posts. There is, we know now to our sorrow, more than one world to be drawn out of nature. When once drawn, like some irreplaceable card in a great game, that world leads on to others. Bacon's "second world" becomes a multiplying forest of worlds in which man's ability to choose is subdued to frightened day-to-day decisions.

One thing, however, becomes ever more apparent: the worlds drawn out of nature are human worlds, and their imperfections stem essentially from human inability to choose intelligently among those contingent and intertwined roads which Bacon hoped would enhance our chances of making a proper and intelligent choice. Instead of regarding man as a corresponding problem, as Bacon's insight suggested, we chose, instead, to concentrate upon that natural world which he truthfully held to be protean, malleable, and capable of human guidance. Although worlds can be drawn out of that maelstrom, they do not always serve the individual imprisoned within the substance of things.

I have often had occasion to comment on the insights of D'Arcy Thompson, the late renowned British naturalist. He saw, long after, in 1897, that with the coming of industrial man, contingency itself is subjected to a kind of increasing tempo of evolution. The simplicity of the rural village of Shakespeare's day, or even the complex but stabilized and harmonious life of a very ancient civilization, is destroyed in the dissonance of excessive and rapid change. "Strike a new note," said Thompson, "import a foreign element to work and a new orbit, and the one accident gives birth to a myriad. Change, in short, breeds change, and chance—chance. We see indeed a sort of *evolution* of chance, an ever-increasing complexity of accident and possibilities. One wave started at the beginning of eternity breaks into component waves, and at once the theory of interference begins to operate." This evolution of chance is not contained within the human domain. Arising within the human orbit it is reflected back into the natural world where man's industrial wastes and destructive experiments increasingly disrupt and unbalance the world of living nature.

Bacon shared in some part with his age a belief in the biform nature of the worldly universe. "There is no nature," he says, "which can be regarded as simple; every one seeming to participate and be compounded of two." Man has something of the brute; the brute has something of the vegetable, the vegetable something of the inanimate body; and so, Bacon emphasizes, "all things are in truth biformed and made up of a higher species and a lower." Strange though it may seem, in this respect Bacon, though existing on the brief Elizabethan stage of a short-term universe, was perhaps better prepared for the protean writhings of external nature and the variability manifest in the interior world of thought than many a specialist in the physical and biological sciences who would follow him.

Patrick Cruttwell, in his study of Shakespeare, comments on how frequently war within the individual, a sense of divided personality, is widespread in the spirit of that age, as it also is in ours:

> "Within my soul there doth conduce a fight
> Of this strange nature, that a thing inseparate,
> Divides more widely than the skie and earth."

How much more we would see, I sometimes think, if the world were lit solely by lightning flashes from the Elizabethan stage. What miraculous insights and perceptions might our senses be trained to receive amidst the alternate crash of thunder and the hurtling force that give a peculiar and momentary shine to an old tree on a wet night. Our world might be transformed interiorly from its staid arrangement of laws and uniformity of expression into one where the unexpected and blinding illumination constituted our faith in reality.

Nor is such a world as incredible as it seems. Physicists, it now appears, are convinced that a principle of uncertainty exists in the submicroscopic realm of particles and that out of this queer domain of accident and impact has emerged, by some kind of mathematical magic, the sustaining world of natural law by which we make our way to the bank, the theater, to our homes, and finally to our graves. Perhaps, after all, a world so created has something still wild and unpredictable lurking behind its more sober manifestations. It is my contention that this is true, and that the rare freedom of the particle to do what most particles never do is duplicated in the solitary universe of the human mind.

The lightning flashes, the smashed circuits through which, on occasion, leaps the light of universes beyond our ken, exist only in rare individuals. But the flashes from such minds can fascinate and light up through the arts of communication the intellects of those not necessarily endowed with genius. In a conformist age science must, for this reason, be wary of its own authority. The individual must be re-created in the light of a revivified humanism which sets the value of man the unique against that vast and ominous shadow of man the composite, the predictable, which is the delight of the machine. The polity we desire is that ever-creative polity which Robert Louis Stevenson had in mind when he spoke of each person as containing a group of incongruous and ofttimes conflicting citizenry. Bacon himself was seeking the road by which the human mind might be opened to the full image of the world, not reduced to the little compass of a state-manipulated machine.

It is through the individual brain alone that there passes the momentary illumination in which a whole human countryside may be transmuted in an instant. "A steep and unaccountable transition," Thoreau has described it, "from what is called a common sense view of things, to an infinitely expanded and liberating one, from seeing things as men describe them, to seeing them as men cannot describe them." Man's mind, like the expanding universe itself, is engaged in pouring over limitless horizons. At its heights of genius it betrays all the miraculous unexpectedness which we try vainly to eliminate from the universe. The great artist, whether he be musician, painter, or poet, is known for this absolute unexpectedness. One does not see, one does not hear, until he speaks to us out of that limitless creativity which is his gift.

The flash of lightning in a single brain also flickers along the horizon of our more ordinary heads. Without that single lightning stroke in a solitary mind, however, the rest of us would never have known the fairyland of *The Tempest*, the midnight world of Dostoevsky, or the blackbirds on the yellow harvest fields of Van Gogh. We would have seen blackbirds and endured the depravity of our own hearts, but it would not be the same landscape that the act of genius transformed. The world without Shakespeare's insights is a lesser world, our griefs shut more inarticulately in upon themselves. We grow mute at the thought—just as an element seems to disappear from sunlight without Van Gogh. Yet these creations we might call particle episodes in the human universe—acts without precedent, a kind of disobedience of normality, unprophesiable by science, unduplicable by other individuals on demand. They are part of that unpredictable newness which keeps the universe from being fully explored by man.

Since this elusive "personality" of the particle may play a role in biological change and diversity, there is a way in which the mysterious world of particles may influence events within the realm of the living. It is just here, within the human domain of infinite variability and the individual act, that the role of the artist lies. Here the creative may be contrasted to the purely scientific approach to nature, although we must bear in mind that a man may be both a scientist and artist—an individual whose esthetic and humanistic interests are as much a part of his greatness in the eyes of the world as the technical skills which have brought him renown.

Ordinarily, however, there is between the two realms a basic division which has been widened in the modern world. Granted that the great scientific discoverer may experience the esthetic joy of the true artist, a substantial difference still remains. For science seeks essentially to naturalize man in the structure of predictable law and conformity, whereas the artist is interested in man the individual.

"This is your star," says science. "Accept the world we describe to you." But the escaping human mind cries out, in the words of G. K. Chesterton, "We have come to the wrong star. . . . That is what makes life at once so splendid and so strange. The true happiness is that we don't fit. We come from somewhere else. We have lost our way."

A few years ago I chanced to write a book in which I had expressed some personal views and feelings upon birds, bones, spiders, and time, all subjects with which I had some degree of acquaintance. Scarcely had the work been published when I was sought out in my office by a serious young colleague. With utter and devastating confidence he had paid me a call in order to correct my deviations and to lead me back to the proper road of scholarship. He pointed out to me the time I had wasted—time which could have been more properly expended upon my own field of scientific investigation. The young man's view of science was a narrow one, but it illustrates a conviction all too common today: namely, that the authority of science is absolute.

To those who have substituted authoritarian science for authoritarian religion, individual thought is worthless unless it is the symbol for a reality which can be seen, tasted, felt, or thought about by everyone else. Such men adhere to a dogma as rigidly as men of fanatical religiosity. They reject the world of the personal, the happy world of open, playful, or aspiring thought.

Here, indeed, we come upon a serious aspect of our discussion. For there is a widespread but totally erroneous impression that science is an unalterable and absolute system. It is supposed that other institutions change, but that science, after the discovery of the scientific method, remains adamant and inflexible in the purity of its basic outlook. This is an iron creed which is at least partly illusory. A very ill-defined thing known as the scientific method persists, but the motivations behind it have altered from century to century.

The science of the seventeenth century, as many historians have pointed out, was essentially theoretical and other-wordly. Its observations revolved largely about a world regarded as under divine control and balance. As we come into the nineteenth century, cosmic and organic evolution begin to effect a change in religious outlook. The rise of technology gave hope for a Baconian Utopia of the New Atlantis model. Problem solving became the rage of science. Today problem solving with mechanical models, even of living societies, continues to be popular. The emphasis, however, has shifted to power. From a theoretical desire to *understand* the universe, we have come to a point where it is felt we *must* understand it to survive. Governments expend billions upon particle research, cosmic-ray research, not because they have been imbued suddenly with a great hunger for truth, but for the very simple, if barbarous, reason that they know the power which lies in the particle. If the physicist learns the nature of the universe in his cyclotron, well and good, but the search is for power.

One period, for reasons of its own, may be interested in stability, another in change. One may prefer morphology, another function. There are styles in science just as in other institutions. The Christianity of today is not totally the Christianity of five centuries ago; neither is science impervious to change. We have lived to see the technological progress that was hailed in one age as the savior of man become the horror of the next. We have observed that the same able and energetic minds which built lights, steamships, and telephones turn with equal facility to the creation of what is euphemistically termed the "ultimate weapon."

It is in this reversal that the modern age comes off so badly. It does so because the forces which have been released have tended to produce an exaggerated conformity and, at the same time, an equally exaggerated assumption that science, a tool for manipulating the outside, the material universe, can be used to create happiness and ethical living. Science can be—and is—used by good men, but in its present sense it can scarcely be said to create them. Science, of course, in discovery represents the individual, but in the moment of triumph, science creates uniformity through which the mind of the individual once more flees away.

It is the part of the artist—the humanist—to defend that eternal flight, just as it is the part of science to seek to impose laws, regularities and certainties. Man desires the certainties but he also transcends them. Thus, as in so many other aspects of life, man inhabits a realm half in and half out of nature, his mind reaching forever beyond the tool, the uniformity, the law, into some realm which is that of mind alone. The pen and the brush represent that eternal search, that conscious recognition of the individual as the unique creature beyond the statistic.

Modern science itself tacitly admits the individual, as in this statement from P. B. Medawar: "We can be sure that, identical twins apart, each human being alive today differs genetically from any other human being; moreover, he is probably different from any other human being who has ever lived or is likely to live in thousands of years to come. The potential variation of human beings is enormously greater than their actual variation; to put it in another way, the ratio of possible men to actual men is overwhelmingly large."

So far does modern science spell out for us that genetic indeterminacy which parallels, in a sense, the indeterminacy of the subatomic particle. Yet all the vast apparatus of modern scientific communication seems fanatically bent upon reducing that indeterminacy as quickly as possible into the mold of rigid order. Programs which do not satisfy in terms of millions vanish from the air. Gone from most of America is the kind of entertainment still to be found in certain of the world's pioneer backlands where a whole village may gather around a little company of visitors. The local musician hurries to the scene, an artist draws pictures to amuse the children, stories are told with gestures across the barrier of tongues, and an enormous release of creative talent goes on into the small hours of the night.

The technology which, in our culture, has released urban and even rural man from the quiet before his hearth log has debauched his taste. Man no longer dreams over a book in which a soft voice, a constant companion, observes, exhorts, or sighs with him through the pangs of youth and age. Today he is more likely to sit before a screen and dream the mass dream which comes from outside.

No one need object to the elucidation of scientific

principles in clear, unornamental prose. What concerns us is the fact that there exists a new class of highly skilled barbarians—not representing the very great in science—who would confine men entirely to this diet. Once more there is revealed the curious and unappetizing puritanism which attaches itself all too readily to those who, without grace or humor, have found their salvation in "facts."

There has always been violence in the world. A hundred years ago the struggle for existence among living things was much written upon and it was popular for even such scholars as Darwin and Wallace to dwell upon the fact that the vanquished died quickly and that the sum of good outweighed the pain. Along with the rising breed of scientific naturalists, however, there arose a different type of men. Stemming from the line of parson naturalists represented by Gilbert White, author of *The Natural History of Selborne*, these literary explorers of nature have left a powerful influence upon English thought. The grim portrait of a starving lark cracking an empty snail shell before Richard Jefferies' window on a bleak winter day is from a world entirely different from that of the scientist. Jefferies' observation is sharp, his facts accurate, yet there is, in his description, a sense of his own poignant hunger—the hunger of a dying man—for the beauty of an earth insensible to human needs. Here again we are in the presence of an artist whose vision is unique.

Even though they were not discoverers in the objective sense, one feels at times that the great nature essayists had more individual perception than their scientific contemporaries. Theirs was a different contribution. They opened the minds of men by the sheer power of their thought. The world of nature, once seen through the eye of genius, is never seen in quite the same manner afterward. A dimension has been added, something that lies beyond the careful analyses of professional biology. Something uncapturable by man passes over W. H. Hudson's vast landscapes. They may be touched with the silvery light from summer thistledown, or bleaker weathers, but always a strange nostalgia haunts his pages—the light of some lost star within his individual mind.

This is a different thing from that which some scientists desire, or that many in the scientific tradition appreciate, but without this rare and exquisite sensitivity to guide us the truth is we are half blind. We will lack pity and tolerance, not through intent, but from blindness. It is within the power of great art to shed on nature a light which can be had from no other source than the mind itself. It was from this doorway, perhaps, that de la Mare's celestial visitant had intruded. Nature, Emerson knew, is "the immense shadow of man." We have cast it in our image. To change nature, mystical though it sounds, we have to change ourselves. We have to draw out of nature that ideal second world which Bacon sought. The modern world is only slowly beginning to realize the profound implications of that idea.

Perhaps we can amplify to some degree certain of our observations concerning man as he is related to the natural world. In Western Europe, for example, there used to be a strange old fear, a fear of mountains, of precipices, of wild untrodden spaces which, to the superstitious heart, seemed to contain a hint of lurking violence or indifference to man. It is as though man has always felt in the presence of great stones and rarified air something that dwarfed his confidence and set his thoughts to circling—an ice age, perhaps, still not outlived in the human mind.

There is a way through this barrier of the past that can be taken by science. It can analyze soil and stones. It can identify bones, listen to the radioactive tick of atoms in the lattices of matter. Science can spin the globe and follow the age-long marchings of man across the wastes of time and space.

Yet if we turn to the pages of the great nature essayists

we may perceive once more the role which the gifted writer and thinker plays in the life of man. Science explores the natural world and thereby enhances our insight, but if we turn to the pages of *The Main Woods,* regarded by critics as one of Henry David Thoreau's minor works, we come upon a mountain ascent quite unparalleled in the annals of literature.

The effect does not lie in the height of the mountain. It does not lie in the scientific or descriptive efforts made on the way up. Instead the cumulative effect is compounded of two things: a style so appropriate to the occasion that it evokes the shape of earth before man's hand had fallen upon it and, second, a terrible and original question posed on the mountain's summit. Somewhere along the road of that spiritual ascent—for it *was* a spiritual as well as a physical ascent—the pure observation gives way to awe, the obscure sense of the holy.

From the estimate of heights, of geological observation, Thoreau enters what he calls a "cloud factory" where mist was generated out of the pure air as fast as it flowed away. Stumbling onward over what he calls "the raw materials of a planet" he comments: "It was vast, titanic, and such as man never inhabits. Some part of the beholder, even some vital part, seems to escape through the loose grating of his ribs as he ascends. His reason is dispersed and shadowy, more thin and subtile, like the air. Vast, inhuman nature has got him at disadvantage, caught him alone, and pilfers him of some of his divine faculty." Thoreau felt himself in the presence of a force "not bound to be kind to man." "What is it," he whispers with awe, "to be admitted to a Museum, compared with being shown some star's surface, some hard matter in its home."

At this moment there enters into his apprehension a new view of substance, the heavy material body he had dragged up the mountain the while something insubstantial seemed to float out of his ribs. Pausing in astonishment, he remarks: "I stand in awe of my body, this matter to which I am bound has become so strange to me. I fear not spirits, ghosts, of which I am one—*that* my body might—but I fear bodies, I tremble to meet them. What is this Titan that has possession of me? Talk of mysteries!— think of our life in nature—daily to be shown matter, to come in contact with it—rocks, trees, wind on our cheeks! the solid earth, the actual world." Over and over he muses, his hands on the huge stones, "Who are we? Where are we?"

The essayist has been struck by an enormous paradox. In that cloud factory of the brain where ideas form as tenuously as mist streaming from mountain rocks, he has glimpsed the truth that mind is locked in matter like the spirit Ariel in a cloven pine. Like Ariel, men struggle to escape the drag of the matter they inhabit, yet it is spirit that they fear. "A Titan grasps us," argues Thoreau, confronting the rocks of the great mountain, a mass solid enough not to be dragged about by the forces of life. "Think of our life in nature," he reiterates. "Who are we?"

From the streaming cloud-wrack of a mountain summit, the voice floats out to us before the fog closes in once more. In that arena of rock and wind we have moved for a moment in a titanic world and hurled at stone titanic questions. We have done so because a slight, gray-eyed man walked up a small mountain which, by some indefinable magic, he transformed into a platform for something, as he put it, "not kind to man."

I do not know in the whole of literature a more penetrating expression of the spirit's horror of the substance it lies trapped within. It is the cry of an individual genius who has passed beyond science into a high domain of cloud. Let it not be forgotten, however, that Thoreau revered and loved true science, and that science and the human spirit together may find a way across that vast mountain whose shadow still looms menacingly above us.

"If you would learn the secrets of nature," Thoreau insisted, "you must practice more humanity than others." It is the voice of a man who loved both knowledge and the humane tradition. His faith has been ill kept within our time.

Mystical truths, however, have a way of knowing neither time nor total death. Many years ago, as an impressionable youth, I found myself lost at evening in a rural and obscure corner of the United States. I was there because of certain curious and rare insects that the place afforded —beetles with armored excrescences, stick insects which changed their coloration like autumn grass. It was a country which, for equally odd and inbred reasons, was the domain of people of similar exuberance of character, as though nature, either physically or mentally, had prepared them for odd niches in a misfit world.

As I passed down a sandy backwoods track where I hoped to obtain directions from a solitary house in the distance, I was overtaken by one of the frequent storms that blow up in that region. The sky turned dark and a splatter of rain struck the ruts of the road. Standing uncertainly at the roadside I heard a sudden rumble over a low plank bridge beyond me. A man high on a great load of hay was bearing down on me through the lowering dark. I could hear through the storm his harsh cries to the horses. I stepped forward to hail him and ask directions. Perhaps he would give me a ride.

There happened then, in a single instant, one of those flame-lit revelations which destroy the natural world forever and replace it with some searing inner vision which accompanies us to the end of our lives. The horses, in the sound and fury of the elements, appeared, even with the loaded rick, to be approaching at a gallop. The dark figure of the farmer with the reins swayed high above them in some limbo of lightning and storm. At that moment I lifted my hand and stepped forward. The horses seemed to pause—even the rain.

Then, in a bolt of light that lit the man on the hayrick, the waste of sodden countryside, and what must have been my own horror-filled countenance, the rain plunged down once more. In that brief, momentary glimpse within the heart of the lightning, haloed, in fact, by its wet shine, I had seen a human face of so incredible a nature as still to amaze and mystify me as to its origin. It was—by some fantastic biological exaggeration—two faces welded vertically together along the midline, like the riveted iron toys of my childhood. One side was lumpish with swollen and malign excrescences; the other shone in the blue light, pale, ethereal, and remote—a face marked by suffering, yet serene and alien to that visage with which it shared this dreadful mortal frame.

As I instinctively shrank back, the great wagon leaped and rumbled on its way to vanish at what spot I knew not. As for me, I offer no explanation for my conduct. Perhaps my eyes deceived me in that flickering and grotesque darkness. Perhaps my mind had spent too long a day on the weird excesses of growth in horned beetles. Nevertheless I am sure that the figure on the hayrick had raised a shielding hand to his own face.

One does not, in youth, arrive at the total meaning of such incidents or the deep symbolism involved in them. Only if the event has been frightening enough, a revelation out of the heavens themselves, does it come to dominate the meaning of our lives. But that I saw the double face of mankind in that instant of vision I can no longer doubt. I saw man—all of us—galloping through a torrential landscape, diseased and fungoid, with that pale half-visage of nobility and despair dwarfed but serene upon a twofold countenance. I saw the great horses with their swaying load plunge down the storm-filled track. I saw, and touched a hand to my own face.

Recently it has been said by a great scientific historian that the day of the literary naturalist is done, that the precision of the laboratory is more and more encroaching upon that individual domain. I am convinced that this is a mistaken judgment. We forget—as Bacon did not forget—that there is a natural history of souls, nay, even of man himself, which can be learned only from the symbolism inherent in the world about him.

It is the natural history that led Hudson to glimpse eternity in some old men's faces at Land's End, that led Thoreau to see human civilizations as toadstools sprung up in the night by solitary roads, or that provoked Melville to experience in the sight of a sperm whale some colossal alien existence without which man himself would be incomplete.

"There is no Excellent Beauty that hath not some strangeness in the Proportion," wrote Bacon in his days of insight. Anyone who has picked up shells on a strange beach can confirm his observation. But man, modern man, who has not contemplated his otherness, the multiplicity of other possible men who dwell or might have dwelt in him, has not realized the full terror and responsibility of existence.

It is through our minds alone that man passes like that swaying furious rider on the hayrick, farther and more desperately into the night. He is galloping—this twofold creature whom even Bacon glimpsed—across the storm-filled heath of time, from the dark world of the natural toward some dawn he seeks beyond the horizon.

Across that midnight landscape he rides with his toppling burden of despair and hope, bearing with him the beast's face and the dream, but unable to cast off either or to believe in either. For he is man, the changeling, in whom the sense of goodness has not perished, nor an eye for some supernatural guidepost in the night.

10

THE CREATURE FROM THE MARSH

I

THE only thing strange about me is my profession. I happen to be one of those few persons who pursue the farther history of man on the planet earth, what Darwin once called "the great subject." But my business is not with the formal art of the history books. Take, for example, today.

Today I have been walking in the ruins of a city. The city still moves, it is true, the air drills ring against iron, and I am aware of laughter and of feet hurrying by at the noon hour. Nevertheless the city is in ruins. This is what the trained eye makes of it. It stands here in the morning sun while rust flakes the steel rails and the leaves of innumerable autumns blow mistily through the ribs of skyscrapers and over the fallen brick work lies a tangle of morning glories. I have seen this before in the dead cities of Mexico—the long centuries wavering past with the curious distortion of things seen through deep sea water. Even the black snake gliding down the steps of the cathedral seems a repetition, past and future being equally resolvable in the curious perspective of the archaeological eye.

But it was not for this that I hurried out to walk in the streets of the city. I wanted to find a symbol, something that would stand for us when the time came, something that might be proud after there was no stone upon another —some work of art, perhaps, or a gay conceit that the rains had not tarnished, something that would tell our story to whatever strange minds might come groping there.

I think I must have walked miles in those ruins. I studied a hundred shop windows. I weighed with a quarter-century of digging experience the lasting qualities of metal, stone, and glass. I hesitated over the noble inscriptions upon public buildings, while the rain dissolved in the locked containers the files of treaties and the betrayal of all human trust. I passed by the signs of coruscating heat and the wilted metal of huge guns. I found the china head of a doll in the metal of a baby carriage that my mind took hold of and considered carefully, though later I realized I stood by a living nursemaid in the Park.

I looked at tools, and at flowers in the windows of tenements. (They will creep out and grow, I thought.) And I heard a dog howl in the waste streets for the comforting hand of man. I saw the vacant, ashy leaves of books blow by, but I did not pick them up. There were dead television screens and the curious detached loneliness of telephone receivers whose broken wires still thrummed in the winds over the Sierra.

It will never do, I thought; there was more to us than this—with all the evil, with all the cruelty. I remembered an inscribed gold ring in a pawnshop window. "From Tom to Mary," it had read, "for always." It is back there, I

thought; that might be it—there was love in us, things we
spoke to each other in the evenings or on deathbeds, the
eyes frank at last. It might be there. I turned and hurried
back.

But the little shop was gone, and finally I came up short
at a place where stones had tumbled in a peculiar way,
half sheltering a fallen window. There were bones there,
and at first this made no sense because bones in exposed
places do not last well, and there are so many of them
finally that the meaning escapes you.

There was a broken sign LED——— Fi———
Av———. And among the bits of glass, a little cluster of
feathers, and under a shattered pane, the delicate bones of
a woman's hand that, dying, had reached wistfully out,
caught there, when the time came.

Why not? I mused. The human hand, the hand is the
story. I touched one of the long, graceful bones. It had
come the evolutionary way up from far eons and watery
abysses only to perish here.

There was a little restless stirring beside me.

So it died after all that effort, I thought on. Five
hundred million years expended in order that the shining
thread of life could die reaching after a little creation of
feathers in the window of a shop. And why not? Even my
antique reptilian eye had a feel for something—a kind of
beauty here . . .

The tugging at my sleeve continued. The slow, affec-
tionate voice of my wife said to me, "Wait here. I want to
go in."

"Of course," I said, and took and squeezed her slender
hand as I returned from some far place. "It will look becoming," I said. "I will stand here and watch."

"The gloves to match it are of green lizard skin," she ex-
ulted.

"That will look just right," I ventured, and did not quite
know what I meant. "I will stand here and watch."

A swinging light like a warning at a railroad crossing began flashing in the darkness below consciousness. A bell began jangling. Then it subsided. My wife was pointing, for the benefit of an attentive clerk, at a little cluster of feathers in the window. I came forward then and beckoned hastily. "But why—?" she said. "Another day," I said, wiping my forehead. It was just that—"Another time," I promised and urged her quickly away.

It is the nature, you see, of the profession—the terrible *déjà vu* of the archaeologist, the memory that scans before and after. For instance, take the case of the black skull, a retreat, some might say, in another direction.

II

The skull was black when they brought it to me. It was black from the irons and acids and mineral replacements of ice-age gravels. It was polished and worn and gleaming from the alterations of unnumbered years. It had made strange journeys after the death of its occupant; it had moved with glacial slowness in the beds of rivers; it had been tumbled by floods and, becoming an object of grisly beauty, had been picked up and passed from hand to hand by men the individual had never seen in life.

Finally it was brought to me.

It was my duty to tell them about the skull.

It was my professional duty to clothe these bones once more with the faint essence of a personality, to speak of a man or a woman, young or old, as the bones might tell the story. It was my task to read the racial features in a forgotten face, stare deep into the hollow sockets through which had once passed in endless procession the days and seasons and the shed tears of long ago.

The woman had been young. I could tell them that. I could tell them she had once fallen or been struck and that after a long time the bone had mended and she had recovered—how, it was difficult to say, for it had been a dangerous and compound fracture. Today such a wound would mean months of immobilization in a hospital. This woman had survived without medical attention through the endless marchings and journeyings of the hunters' world. Even the broken orbit of the left eye had dropped by a quarter of an inch—a serious disfigurement. Nevertheless she had endured and lived on toward some doom that had come fast upon her but was not written in the bones. It was, in all likelihood, a death by violence. Her skull had not been drawn from a grave. It had come from beneath the restless waters of a giant river that is known to keep its secrets well.

They asked me for the time of these events, and again, obediently, I went down that frail ladder which stretches below us into the night of time. I went slowly, by groping deductions and the hesitant intuitions of long experience that only scholars know. I passed through ages where water was wearing away the shapes of river pebbles into crystalline sand and the only sound in the autumn thickets was the gathering of south-flying birds. Somewhere in the neighborhood of the five thousandth millennium—I could place it no closer than that—the ladder failed me. The river was still there but larger—an enormous rolling waste of water and marshes out of which rose a vast October moon.

They interrupted me then, querulously, asking if archaeologists could do no better than this, and was it not true that there were new and clever methods by which physicists could call the year in the century and mark the passage of time by the tick of atoms in the substance of things. And I said, yes, within limits it was true, but that the methods were not always usable, and that the subtle contaminations possible among radioactive objects sometimes defeated our attempts.

At this point they shook their heads unwillingly, for, as
I quickly saw, they had the passion of modern men for the
precision of machines and disliked vagueness of any sort.
But the skull lay there on the table between us, and over it
one man lingered, fascinated in spite of himself. I knew
what he was thinking: Where am I going? When shall I
become like this?

I heard this in his mind for just an instant while I stared
across at him from among my boxes of teeth and flint arrowheads that had grown chalky and dull with the passage
of long centuries in the ground.

"Thank you," the visitor said finally, moving after his
party to the door. He was, I saw, unsure for what it was
he thanked me.

"You are quite welcome," I said, still returning slowly
from that waste of forgotten water over which the birds of
another century cried dolefully, so that I could hear them
keening in my head. Like the man who asks a medium to
bring back some whimpering memoryless ghost and make
it speak out of a living mouth for the amusement of a
group of curiosity seekers, he may have felt remorse. At
any rate, he nodded uncertainly and fled.

I was the instrument. I had made this journey a
hundred times for students who scrawled their initials on
my skulls, a hundred times for reporters who wanted sen-
sational accounts of monkey-men, a hundred times for
people who came up at the end of lectures and asked,
"How much money are the bones worth, doctor? Are they
easy to find?"

In spite of this I have continued to make these journeys.
It is old habit now. I go back into the past alone. I would
do so if I fled my job and sought safety in some obscure
room. My sense of time is so heightened that I can feel the
frost at work in stones, the first creeping advance of grass
in a deserted street. I have stood by the carved sarcophagi
of dead knights in a European cathedral, men seven

hundred years away from us with their steel and their ladies, and from that point striven to hurl the mind still backward into the wilderness where man coughs bestially and vanishes into the shape of beasts.

No, I cannot say I am a student of the dates in the history books. My life is mostly occupied with caves filled up and drifted over with the leaves of ten thousand thousand autumns. My specialty is the time when man was changing into man. But, like a river that twists, evades, hesitates through slow miles, and then leaps violently down over a succession of cataracts, man can be called a crisis animal. Crisis is the most powerful element in his definition. Of his entire history, this he understands the least. Only man has continued to turn his own definition around upon his tongue until, in the end, he has looked outside of nature to something invisible to any eye but his own. Long ago, this emotion was well expressed in the Old Testament. "Oh Lord," exclaimed the prophet Jeremiah, "I know that the way of man is not in himself." Therefore, I would add, as a modern evolutionist, "the way" only lies through man and has to be sought beyond him. It was this that led to a very remarkable experience.

III

"The greatest prize of all," once confessed the British plant explorer F. Kingdon Ward, "is the skull of primitive man." Ward forgot one thing: there are other clues to primitive men than those confined to skulls. The bones of fossil men are few because the earth tolerated them in scant numbers. We call them missing links on the road to ourselves. A little less tooth here, a little more brain there, and you can see them changing toward ourselves in that long historyless time when the great continental ice sheets ebbed and flowed across the northern continents. Like all the students of that age, I wanted to find a missing link in human history. That is what this record is about, for I stumbled on the track of one.

Some men would maintain that a vague thing called atmosphere accounts for such an episode as I am about to relate, that there are houses that demand a murder and wait patiently until the murderer and his victim arrive, that there are great cliffs that draw the potential suicide from afar or mountains of so austere a nature that they write their message on the face of a man who looks up at them. This all may be. I do not deny it. But when I encountered the footprint in the mud of that remote place I think the thing that terrified me most was the fact that I knew to whom it belonged and yet I did not want to know him. He was a stranger to me and remains so to this day. Because of a certain knowledge I had, however, he succeeded in impressing himself upon me in a most insidious manner. I have never been the same since the event took place, and often at night I start up sweating and think uncannily that the creature is there with me in the dark. If the sense of his presence grows, I switch on the light, but I never look into the mirror. This is a matter of old habit with me.

First off, though, we must get straight what we mean by a missing link.

A missing link is a day in the life of a species that is changing its form and habits, just as, on a smaller scale, one's appearance and behavior at the age of five are a link in one's development to an adult man or woman. The individual person may have changed and grown, but still the boy or girl of many years ago is linked to the present by a long series of steps. And if one is really alive and not already a living fossil, one will go on changing till the end of one's life and perhaps be the better for it. The term "missing link" was coined because some of the physical links in the history of man as a species are lost, and those people who, like myself, are curious about the past look for them.

My album is the earth, and the pictures in it are faded and badly torn and have to be pieced together by detective work. If one thinks of oneself at five years of age, one may get a thin wisp of disconnected memory pictures. By contrast, the past of a living species is without memory except as that past has written its physical record in vestigial organs like the appendix or a certain pattern on our molar teeth. To eke out what those physical stigmata tell us, we have to go grubbing about in caves and gravel for the bones of very ancient men. If one can conceive of the trouble an archaeologist might have in locating one's remains a half-million years from now, supposing they still existed, one will get an idea of the difficulties involved in finding traces of man before his bones were crowded together in cities and cemeteries.

I was wandering inland along a sunken shore when the thing happened—the thing I had dreamed of so long. In other words, I got a clue to man. The beaches on that coast I had come to visit are treacherous and sandy and the tides are always shifting things about among the mangrove roots. It is not a place to which I would willingly return and you will get no bearings from me. Anyway, what it was I found there could be discovered on any man's coast if he looked sharp for it. I had come to that place with other things in mind, and a notion of being alone. I was tired. I wanted to lie in the sun or clamber about like an animal in the swamps and the forest. To secure such rest from the turmoil of a modern city is the most difficult thing in the world to accomplish and I have only achieved it twice: once in one of the most absolute deserts in the world and again in this tropical marsh.

By day and night strange forms of life scuttled and gurgled underfoot or oozed wetly along outthrust branches; luminous tropical insects blundered by in the dark like the lamps of hesitant burglars. Overhead, on higher ground, another life shrieked distantly or was expectantly still in the treetops. Somehow, alone as I was, I got to listening as if all that world were listening, waiting for something to happen. The trees drooped a little lower listening, the tide lurked and hesitated on the beach, and even a tree snake dropped a loop and hung with his face behind a spider web, immobile in the still air.

A world like that is not really natural, or (the thought strikes one later) perhaps it really is, only more so. Parts of it are neither land nor sea and so everything is moving from one element to another, wearing uneasily the queer transitional bodies that life adopts in such places. Fish, some of them, come out and breathe air and sit about watching you. Plants take to eating insects, mammals go back to the water and grow elongate like fish, crabs climb trees. Nothing stays put where it began because everything is constantly climbing in, or climbing out, of its unstable environment.

Along drowned coasts of this variety you only see, in a sort of speeded-up way, what is true of the whole world and everything upon it: the Darwinian world of passage, of missing links, of beetles with soldered, flightless wings, of snakes with vestigial feet dragging slowly through the underbrush. Everything is marred and maimed and slightly out of focus—everything in the world. As for man, he is no different from the rest. His back aches, he ruptures easily, his women have difficulties in childbirth—all because he has struggled up upon his hind legs without having achieved a perfect adjustment to his new posture.

On this particular afternoon, I came upon a swamp full of huge waterlilies where I had once before ventured. The wind had begun to rise and rain was falling at intervals. As far as I could see, giant green leaves velvetly impervious to water were rolling and twisting in the wind. It was a species of lily in which part of the leaves projected on stalks for a short distance above the water, and as they rolled and tossed the whole swamp flashed and quivered from the innumerable water drops that were rolling around and around like quicksilver in the great cupped leaves. Everything seemed flickering and changing as if in some gigantic illusion, but so soft was the green light and so delicate the brushing of the leaves against each other that the whole effect was quite restful, as though one could be assured that nothing was actually tangible or real and no one in his senses would want it to be, as long as he could sway and nod and roll reflecting water drops about over the surface of his brain.

Just as I finally turned away to climb a little ridge I found the first footprint. It was in a patch of damp, exposed mud and was pointed away from the water as though the creature had emerged directly out of the swamp and was heading up the shore toward the interior. I had thought I was alone, and in that place it was wise to know one's neighbors. Worst of all, as I stood studying the footprint, and then another, still heading up the little rise, it struck me that though undoubtedly human the prints were different in some indefinable way. I will tell you once more that this happened on the coast of another country in a place where form itself is an illusion and no shape of man or beast is totally impossible. I crouched anxiously in the mud while all about the great leaves continued to rotate on their stems and to flash their endlessly rolling jewels.

But there were these footprints. They did not disappear. As I fixed the lowermost footprint with every iota of scientific attention I could muster, it became increasingly apparent that I was dealing with some transitional form of man. The arch, as revealed in the soft mud, was low and flat and implied to the skilled eye an inadequate adjustment to the upright posture. This, in its turn, suggested certain things about the spine and the nature of the skull. It was only then, I think, that the full import of my discovery came to me.

Good Lord, I thought consciously for the first time, the thing is alive. I had spent so many years analyzing the bones of past ages or brooding over lizard tracks turned to stone in remote epochs that I had never contemplated this possibility before. The thing was alive and it was human. I looked uneasily about before settling down into the mud once more. One could make out that the prints were big but what drew my fascinated eye from the first was the nature of the second toe. It was longer than the big toe, and as I crawled excitedly back and forth between the two wet prints in the open mud, I saw that there was a remaining hint of prehensile flexibility about them.

Most decidedly, as a means of ground locomotion this foot was transitional and imperfect. Its loose, splayed aspect suggested inadequate protection against sprains. That second toe was unnecessarily long for life on the ground, although the little toe was already approximating the rudimentary condition so characteristic of modern man. Could it be that I was dealing with an unreported living fossil, an archaic ancestral survival? What else could be walking the mangrove jungle with a foot that betrayed clearly the marks of ancient intimacy with the arboreal attic, an intimacy so long continued that now, after hundreds of thousands of years of ground life, the creature had squiggled his unnecessarily long toes about in the mud as though an opportunity to clutch at something had delighted his secret soul.

I crouched by the footprint and thought. I remembered that comparisons with the living fauna, whenever available, are good scientific procedure and a great aid to precise taxonomy. I sat down and took off my shoes.

I had never had much occasion to look critically at my own feet before. In modern man they are generally encased in shoes—something that still suggests a slight imperfection in our adaptations. After all, we don't normally find it necessary to go about with our hands constantly enclosed in gloves. As I sat contemplating and comparing my feet with the footprints, a faintly disturbing memory floated hazily across my mind. It had involved a swimming party many years before at the home of one of the most distinguished comparative anatomists in the world. As we had sat on the bench alongside his pool, I had glanced up suddenly and caught him staring with what had seemed unnecessary fascination at my feet. I remembered now that he had blushed a deep pink under his white hair and had diverted my inquiring glance deftly to the scenery about us.

Why I should have remembered the incident at all was unclear to me. I thought of the possibility of getting plaster casts of a footprint, and I also debated whether I should attempt to trail the creature farther up the slope toward which he appeared to have been headed. It was no moment for hesitation. Still, I did hesitate. The uneasy memory grew stronger, and a thought finally struck me. A little sheepishly and with a glance around to see that I was not observed, I lowered my own muddy foot into the footprint. It fitted.

I stood there contemplatively clutching, but this time consciously, the mud in my naked toes. I was the dark being on that island shore whose body carried the marks of its strange passage. I was my own dogging Man Friday, the beast from the past who had come with weapons through the marsh. The wind had died and the green leaves with their rolling jewels were still. The mistake I had made was the mistake of all of us.

The story of man was not all there behind us in the caves of remote epochs. Even our physical bodies gave evidence that the change was not completed. As for our minds, they were still odd compounds of beast and saint.

But it was not by turning back toward the marsh out of which we had come that the truly human kingdom was to be possessed and entered—that kingdom dreamed of in many religions and spoken of in many barbarous tongues. A philosopher once said in my presence, "The universe is a series of leaping sparks—everything else is interpretation." But what, I hesitated, was man's interpretation to be?

I drew a foot out of the little steaming swamp that sucked at it. The air hung heavily about me. I listened as the first beast might have listened who came from the water up the shore and did not return again to his old element. Everything about me listened in turn and seemed to be waiting for some decision on my part. I swayed a moment on my unstable footing.

Then, warily, I stepped higher up the shore and let the water and the silt fill in that footprint to make it, a hundred million years away, a fossil sign of an unknown creature slipping from the shadows of a marsh toward something else that awaited him. I had found the missing link. He walked on misshapen feet. The stones hurt him and his belly sagged. There were dreams like Christmas ornaments in his head, intermingled with an ancient malevolent viciousness. I knew because I was the missing link, but for the first time I sensed where I was going.

I have said I never look into the mirror. It is a matter of old habit now. If that other presence grows too oppressive I light the light and read.

11

ONE NIGHT'S DYING

THERE is always a soft radiance beyond the bedroom door from a night-light behind my chair. I have lived this way for many years now. I sleep or I do not sleep, and the light makes no difference except if I wake. Then, as I awaken, the dim forms of objects sustain my grip on reality. The familiar chair, the walls of the book-lined study reassert my own existence.

I do not lie and toss with doubt any longer, as I did in earlier years. I get up and write, as I am writing now, or I read in the old chair that is as worn as I am. I read philosophy, metaphysics, difficult works that sometime, soon or late, draw a veil over my eyes so that I drowse in my chair.

It is not that I fail to learn from these midnight examinations of the world. It is merely that I choose that examination to remain as remote and abstruse as possible. Even so, I cannot always prophesy the result. An obscure line may whirl me into a wide-awake, ferocious concentration in which ideas like animals leap at me out of the dark, in which sudden odd trains of thought drive me inexorably to my desk and paper. I am, in short, a victim of insomnia— sporadic, wearing, violent, and melancholic. In the words of Shakespeare, for me the world "does murder sleep." It has been so since my twentieth year.

In that year my father died—a man well loved, the mainstay of our small afflicted family. He died slowly in severe bodily torture. My mother was stone-deaf. I, his son, saw and heard him die. We lived in a place and time not free with the pain-alleviating drugs of later decades. When the episode of many weeks' duration was over, a curious thing happened: I could no longer bear the ticking of the alarm clock in my own bedroom.

At first I smothered it with an extra blanket in a box beside my cot, but the ticking persisted as though it came from my own head. I used to lie for hours staring into the dark of the sleeping house, feeling the loneliness that only the sleepless know when the queer feeling comes that it is the sleeping who are alive and those awake are disembodied ghosts. Finally, in desperation, I gave up the attempt to sleep and turned to reading, though it was difficult to concentrate.

It was then that human help appeared. My grandmother saw the light burning through the curtains of my door and came to sit with me. A few years later, when I touched her hair in farewell at the beginning of a journey from which I would not return to see her alive, I knew she had saved my sanity. Into that lonely room at midnight she had come, abandoning her own sleep, in order to sit with one in trouble. We had not talked much, but we had sat together by the lamp, reasserting our common humanity before the great empty dark that is the universe.

Grandmother knew nothing of psychiatry. She had not

reestablished my sleep patterns, but she had done something more important. She had brought me out of a dark room and retied my thread of life to the living world. Henceforward, by night or day, though I have been subject to the moods of depression or gaiety which are a part of the lives of all of us, I have been able not merely to endure but to make the best of what many regard as an unbearable affliction.

It is true that as an educational administrator I can occasionally be caught nodding in lengthy committee meetings, but so, I have observed, can men who come from sound nights on their pillows. Strangely, I, who frequently grow round-eyed and alert as an owl at the stroke of midnight, find it pleasant to nap in daylight among friends. I can roll up on a couch and sleep peacefully while my wife and chatting friends who know my peculiarities keep the daytime universe safely under control. Or so it seems. For, deep-seated in my subconscious, is perhaps the idea that the black bedroom door is the gateway to the tomb.

I try in that bedroom to sleep high on two pillows, to have ears and eyes alert. Something shadowy has to be held in place and controlled. At night one has to sustain reality without help. One has to hear lest hearing be lost, see lest sight not return to follow moonbeams across the floor, touch lest the sense of objects vanish. Oh, sleeping, soundlessly sleeping ones, do you ever think who knits your universe together safely from one day's memory to the next? It is the insomniac, not the night policeman on his beat.

Many will challenge this point of view. They will say that electric power does the trick, that many a roisterer stumbles down the long street at dawn, after having served his purpose of holding the links of the mad world together. There are parts of the nighttime world, men say to me, that it is just as well I do not know. Go home and sleep, man. Others will keep your giddy world together. Let the thief pass quickly in the shadow, he is awake. Let the juvenile gangs which sidle like bands of evil crabs up from the dark waters of poverty into prosperous streets pass without finding you at midnight.

The advice is good, but in the city or the country small things important to our lives have no reporter except as he who does not sleep may observe them. And that man must be disencumbered of reality. He must have no commitments to the dark, as do the murderer and thief. Only he must see, though what he sees may come from the night side of the planet that no man knows well. For even in the early dawn, while men lie unstirring in their sleep or stumble sleepy-eyed to work, some single episode may turn the whole world for a moment into the place of marvel that it is, but that we grow too day-worn to accept.

For example, I call the place where I am writing now the bay of broken things. In the February storms, spume wraiths climb the hundred-foot cliff to fight and fall like bitter rain in the moonlight upon the cabin roof. The earth shakes from the drum roll of the surf. I lie awake and watch through the window beyond my bed. This is no ticking in my brain; this is the elemental night of chaos. This is the sea chewing its million-year way into the heart of the continent.

The caves beneath the cliff resound with thunder. Again those warring wraiths shoot high over the house. Impelled as though I were a part of all those leaping ghosts, I dress in the dark and come forth. With my back against the door, like an ancient necromancer, I hurl my mind into the white spray and try to summon back, among those leaping forms, the faces and features of the dead I know. The shapes rise endlessly, but they pass inland before the wind, indifferent to my mortal voice.

I walk a half mile to a pathway that descends upon a little beach. Below me is a stretch of white sand. No shell is ever found unbroken, even on quiet days, upon that shore. Everything comes over the rocks to seaward. Wood is riven into splinters; the bones of seamen and of sea lions are pounded equally into white and shining sand. Throughout the night the long black rollers, like lines of frothing cavalry, form ranks, drum towering forward, and fall, fall till the mind is dizzy with the spume that fills it. I wait in the shelter of a rock for daybreak. At last the sea eases a trifle. The tide is going out.

I stroll shivering along the shore, and there, exposed in inescapable nakedness, I see the elemental cruelty of the natural world. A broken-winged gull, hurled by the wind against the cliff, runs before me wearily along the beach. It will starve or, mercifully, the dogs will find it. I try not to hurry it, and walk on. A little later in a quieter bend of the shore, I see ahead of me a bleeding, bedraggled blot on the edge of the white surf. As I approach, it starts warily to its feet. We look at each other. It is a wild duck, also with a shattered wing. It does not run ahead of me like the longer-limbed gull. Before I can cut off its retreat it waddles painfully from its brief refuge into the water.

The sea continues to fall heavily. The duck dives awkwardly, but with long knowledge and instinctive skill, under the fall of the first two inshore waves. I see its head working seaward. A long green roller, far taller than my head, rises and crashes forward. The black head of the waterlogged duck disappears. This is the way wild things die, without question, without knowledge of mercy in the universe, knowing only themselves and their own pathway to the end. I wonder, walking farther up the beach, if the man who shot that bird will die as well.

This is the chaos before man came, before sages imbued with pity walked the earth. Indeed it is true, and in my faraway study my hands have often touched with affection the backs of the volumes which line my shelves. Nevertheless, I have endured the nights and mornings of the city. I have seen old homeless men who have slept for hours sitting upright on ledges along the outer hallway of one of the great Eastern stations straighten stiffly in the dawn and limp away with feigned businesslike aloofness before the approach of the policeman on his rounds. I know that on these cold winter mornings sometimes a man, like the pigeons I have seen roosting as closely as possible over warm hotel air vents, will fall stiffly and not awaken. It is true that there are shelters for the homeless, but some men, like their ice-age forebears, prefer their independence to the end.

The loneliness of the city was brought home to me one early sleepless morning, not by men like me tossing in lonely rooms, not by poverty and degradation, not by old men trying with desperate futility to be out among others in the great roaring hive, but by a single one of those same pigeons which I had seen from my hotel window, looking down at midnight upon the smoking air vents and chimneys.

The pigeon, *Columba livia,* is the city bird *par excellence.* He is a descendant of the rock pigeon that in the Old World lived among the cliffs and crevices above the caves that early man inhabited. He has been with us since our beginning and has adapted as readily as ourselves to the artificial cliffs of man's first cities. He has known the Roman palaces and the cities of Byzantium. His little flat feet, suited to high and precarious walking, have sauntered in the temples of vanished gods as readily as in New York's old Pennsylvania Station. In my dim morning strolls, waiting for the restaurants to open, I have seen him march quickly into the back end of a delivery truck while the driver was inside a store engaged in his orders with the proprietor. Yet for all its apparent tolerance of these highly adapted and often comic birds, New York also has a beach of broken things more merciless than the reefs and rollers of the ocean shore.

One morning, strolling sleepless as usual toward early breakfast time in Manhattan, I saw a sick pigeon huddled at an uncomfortable slant against a building wall on a street corner. I felt sorry for the bird, but I had no box, no instrument of help, and had learned long ago that pursuing wounded birds on city streets is a hopeless, dangerous activity. Pigeons, like men, die in scores every day in New York. As I hesitantly walked on, however, I wondered why the doomed bird was assuming such a desperately contorted position under the cornice that projected slightly over it.

At this moment I grew aware of something I had heard more loudly in European streets as the factory whistles blew, but never in such intensity as here, even though American shoes are built of softer materials. All around me the march of people was intensifying. It was New York on the way to work. Space was shrinking before my eyes. The tread of innumerable feet passed from an echo to the steady murmuring of a stream, then to a drumming. A dreadful robot rhythm began to rack my head, a sound like the boots of Nazis in their heyday of power. I was carried along in an irresistible surge of bodies.

A block away, jamming myself between a waste-disposal basket and a lightpost, I managed to look back. No one hesitated at that corner. The human tide pressed on, jostling and pushing. My bird had vanished under that crunching, multi-footed current as remorselessly as the wounded duck under the indifferent combers of the sea. I watched this human ocean, of which I was an unwilling droplet, rolling past, its individual faces like whitecaps passing on a night of storm, fixed, merciless, indifferent; man in the mass marching like the machinery of which he is already a replaceable part, toward desks, computers, missiles, and machines, marching like the waves toward his own death with a conscious ruthlessness no watery shore could ever duplicate. I have never returned to search in that particular street for the face of humanity. I prefer the endlessly rolling pebbles of the tide, the moonstones polished by the pulling moon.

And yet, plunged as I am in dire memories and midnight reading, I have said that it is the sufferer from insomnia who knits the torn edges of men's dreams together in the hour before dawn. It is he who from his hidden, winter vantage point sees the desperate high-hearted bird fly through the doorway of the grand hotel while the sleepy doorman nods, a deed equivalent in human terms to that of some starving wretch evading Peter at heaven's gate, and an act, I think, very likely to be forgiven.

It is a night more mystical, however, that haunts my memory. Around me I see again the parchment of old books and remember how, on one rare evening, I sat in the shadows while a firefly flew from volume to volume lighting its small flame, as if in literate curiosity. Choosing the last title it had illuminated, I came immediately upon these words from St. Paul: "Beareth all things, believeth all things, hopeth all things, endureth all things." In this final episode I shall ask you to bear with me and also to believe.

I sat, once more in the late hours of darkness, in the airport of a foreign city. I was tired as only both the sufferer from insomnia and the traveler can be tired. I had missed a plane and had almost a whole night's wait before me. I could not sleep. The long corridor was deserted. Even the cleaning women had passed by.

In that white efficient glare I grew ever more depressed and weary. I was tired of the endless comings and goings of my profession; I was tired of customs officers and police. I was lonely for home. My eyes hurt. I was, unconsciously perhaps, looking for that warm stone, that hawthorn leaf, where, in the words of the poet, man trades in at last his wife and friend. I had an ocean to cross; the effort seemed unbearable. I rested my aching head upon my hand.

Later, beginning at the far end of that desolate corridor, I saw a man moving slowly toward me. In a small corner of my eye I merely noted him. He limped, painfully and grotesquely, upon a heavy cane. He was far away, and it was no matter to me. I shifted the unpleasant mote out of my eye.

But, after a time, I could still feel him approaching, and in one of those white moments of penetration which are so dreadful, my eyes were drawn back to him as he came on. With an anatomist's eye I saw this amazing conglomeration of sticks and broken, misshapen pulleys which make up the body of man. Here was an apt subject, and I flew to a raging mental dissection. How could anyone, I contended, trapped in this mechanical thing of joints and sliding wires expect the acts it performed to go other than awry?

The man limped on, relentlessly.

How, oh God, I entreated, did we become trapped within this substance out of which we stare so hopelessly upon our own eventual dissolution? How for a single minute could we dream or imagine that thought would save us, children deliver us, from the body of this death? Not in time, my mind rang with my despair; not in mortal time, not in this place, not anywhere in the world would blood be staunched, or the dark wrong be forever righted, or the parted be rejoined. Not in this time, not mortal time. The substance was too gross, our utopias bought with too much pain.

The man was almost upon me, breathing heavily, lunging and shuffling upon his cane. Though an odor emanated from him, I did not draw back. I had lived with death too many years. And then this strange thing happened, which I do not mean physically and cannot explain. The man entered me. From that moment I saw him no more. For a moment I was contorted within his shape, and then out of his body—our bodies, rather—

there arose some inexplicable sweetness of union, some understanding between spirit and body which I had never before experienced. Was it I, the joints and pulleys only, who desired this peace so much?

I limped with growing age as I gathered up my luggage. Something of that terrible passer lingered in my bones, yet I was released, the very room had dilated. As I went toward my plane the words the firefly had found for me came automatically to my lips. "Beareth all things," believe, believe. It is thus that one day and the next are welded together, that one night's dying becomes tomorrow's birth. I, who do not sleep, can tell you this.

12

OBITUARY OF
A BONE HUNTER

I

THE papers and the magazines reprint the stories endlessly these days—of Sybaris the sin city, or, even further back, that skull at Tepexpan. One's ears are filled with chatter about assorted magnetometers and how they are used to pick up the traces of buried objects and no one has to guess at all. They unearth the city, or find the buried skull and bring it home. Then everyone concerned is famous overnight.

I'm the man who didn't find the skull. I'm the man who'd just been looking twenty years for something like it. This isn't sour grapes. It's their skull and welcome to it. What made me sigh was the geophysics equipment. The greatest gambling game in the world—the greatest wit-sharpener—and now they do it with amplifiers and elec-

tronically mapped grids. An effete age, gentlemen, and the
fun gone out of it.

There are really two kinds of bone hunters—the big
bone hunters and the little bone hunters. The little bone
hunters may hunt big bones, but they're little bone hunters
just the same. They are the consistent losers in the most
difficult game of chance that men can play: the search for
human origins. Eugène Dubois, the discoverer of Pithecan-
thropus, hit the jackpot in a gamble with such stupendous
odds that the most devoted numbers enthusiast would
have had better sense than to stake his life on them.

I am a little bone hunter. I've played this game for a
twenty-year losing streak. I used to think it all lay in the
odds—that it was luck that made the difference between
the big and little bone hunters. Now I'm not so sure any
longer. Maybe it's something else.

Maybe sometimes an uncanny clairvoyance is involved,
and if it comes you must act or the time goes by. Anyhow
I've thought about it a lot in these later years. You think
that way as you begin to get grayer and you see pretty
plainly that the game is not going to end as you planned.

With me I think now that there were three chances: the
cave of spiders, the matter of the owl's egg, and the old
man out of the Golden Age. I muffed them all. And maybe
the old man just came to show me I'd sat in the big game
for the last time.

II

In that first incident of the spiders, I was playing a
hunch, a long one, but a good one still. I wanted to find
Neanderthal man, or any kind of ice-age man, in America.
One or two important authorities were willing to admit he
might have got in before the last ice sheet; that he *might*
have crossed Bering Strait with the mammoth. He

might have, they said, but it wasn't likely. And if he had, it would be like looking for hummingbirds in the Bronx to find him.

Well, the odds were only a hundred to one against me, so I figured I'd look. That was how I landed in the cave of spiders. It was somewhere west out of Carlsbad, New Mexico, in the Guadalupe country. Dry. With sunlight that would blister cactus. We were cavehunting with a dynamiter and a young Harvard assistant. The dynamiter was to blow boulders away from fallen entrances so we could dig what lay underneath.

We found the cave up a side canyon, the entrance blocked with fallen boulders. Even to my youthful eyes it looked old, incredibly old. The waters and the frost of centuries had eaten at the boulders and gnawed the cave roof. Down by the vanished stream bed a little gleam of worked flints caught our eye.

We stayed there for days, digging where we could and leaving the blasting till the last. We got the Basket Maker remains we had come to get—the earliest people that the scientists of that time would concede had lived in the Southwest. Was there anything more? We tamped a charge under one huge stone that blocked the wall of the cave and scrambled for the outside. A dull boom echoed down the canyon and the smoke and dust slowly blew away.

Inside the cave mouth the shattered boulder revealed a crack behind it. An opening that ran off beyond our spot lights. The hackles on my neck crawled. This might be the road to—something earlier? There was room for only one man to worm his way in. The dynamiter was busy with his tools. "It's probably nothing," I said to the assistant. "I'll just take a quick look."

As I crawled down that passage on my belly I thought once or twice about rattlesnakes and what it might be like to meet one on its own level where it could look you in the eye. But after all I had met snakes before in this country, and besides I had the feeling that there was something worth getting to beyond.

I had it strong—too strong to turn back. I twisted on and suddenly dropped into a little chamber. My light shot across it. It was low and close, and this was the end of the cave. But there was earth on the floor beneath me, the soft earth that must be dug, that might hold something more ancient than the cave entrance. I couldn't stand up; the roof was too low. I would have to dig on hands and knees. I set the light beside me and started to probe the floor with a trench shovel. It was just then that the fear got me.

The light lay beside me shining on the ceiling—a dull, velvety-looking ceiling, different from the stone around. I don't know when I first sensed that something was wrong, that the ceiling was moving, that waves were passing over it like the wind in a stand of wheat. But suddenly I did; suddenly I dropped the shovel and thrust the light closer against the roof. Things began to detach themselves and drop wherever the light touched them. Things with legs. I could hear them plop on the soft earth around me.

I shut off the light. The plopping ceased. I sat on my knees in the darkness, listening. My mind was centered on just one thing—escape. I knew what that wavering velvet wall was. Millions upon millions of daddy-long-legs— packed in until they hung in layers. Daddy-long-legs, the most innocent and familiar of all the spider family. I wish I could say I had seen black widows there among them. It would help now, in telling this.

But I didn't. I didn't really see anything. If I turned on the light that hideous dropping and stirring would commence again. The light woke them. They disliked it.

If I could have stood up it would have been different. If they had not been overhead it would have been different. But they had me on my knees and they were above and all around. Millions upon millions. How they got there I don't know. All I know is that up out of the instinctive well of my being flowed some ancient, primal fear of the crawler, the walker by night. One clambered over my hand. And above they dangled, dangled. . . . What if they all began to drop at once?

I did not light the light. I had seen enough. I buttoned my jacket close, and my sleeves. I plunged blindly back up the passage down which I had wriggled and which, luckily, was free of them.

Outside the crew looked at me. I was sweating, and a little queer. "Close air," I gasped; "a small hole, nothing there."

We went away then in our trucks. I suppose in due time the dust settled, and the fox found his way in. Probably all that horrible fecund mass eventually crept, in its single individualities, back into the desert where it frightened no one. What it was doing there, what evil unknown to mankind it was plotting, I do not know to this day. The evil and the horror, I think now, welled out of my own mind, but somehow that multitude of ancient life in a little low dark chamber touched it off. It did not pass away until I could stand upright again. It was a fear out of the old, four-footed world that sleeps within us still.

Neanderthal man? He might have been there. But I was young and that was only a first chance gone. Yes, there were things I might have done, but I didn't do them. You don't tell your chief dynamiter that you ran from a daddy-long-legs. Not in that country. But do you see, it wasn't *one* daddy-long-legs. That's what I can't seem to make clear to anyone. It wasn't just one daddy-long-legs. It was millions of them. Enough to bury you. And have you ever thought of being buried under spiders? I thought not. You begin to get the idea?

III

I had a second chance and again it was in a cave I found. This time I was alone, tramping up a canyon watching for bones, and I just happened to glance upward in the one place where the cave could be seen. I studied it a long time—until I could feel the chill crawling down my back. This might be it; this might be the place. . . . This time I would know. This time there would be no spiders.

Through the glasses I could make out a fire-blackened roof, a projecting ledge above the cave mouth, and another one below. It was a small, strange hide-out, difficult to reach, but it commanded the valley on which the canyon opened. And there was the ancient soot-impregnated cave roof. Ancient men had been there.

I made that climb. Don't ask me how I did it. Probably there had been an easier route ages ago. But I came up a naked chimney of rock down which I lost my knapsack and finally the geologist's pick that had helped me hack out a foothold in the softening rock.

When I flung myself over the ledge where the cave mouth opened, I was shaking from the exhausting muscle tension and fear. No one, I was sure, had come that way for a thousand years, and no one after me would come again. I did not know how I would get down. It was enough momentarily to be safe. In front of me the cave mouth ran away darkly into the mountain.

I took the flashlight from my belt and loosened my sheath knife. I began to crawl downward and forward, wedging myself over sticks and fallen boulders. It was a clean cave and something was there, I was sure of it. Only, the walls were small and tight. . . .

They were tighter when the voice and the eyes came. I remember the eyes best. I caught them in my flashlight the same instant that I rammed my nose into the dirt and covered my head. They were big eyes and coming my way.

I never thought at all. I just lay there dazed while a great roaring buffeting thing beat its way out over my body and went away.

It went out into the silence beyond the cave mouth. A half minute afterward, I peered through my fingers and rolled weakly over. Enough is enough. But this time I wasn't going back empty-handed. Not I. Not on account of a mere bird. Not if I *had* thought it was a mountain lion, which it could just as well have been. No owl was going to stop me, not even if it was the biggest owl in the Rocky Mountains.

I twitched my ripped shirt into my pants and crawled on. It wasn't much farther. Over the heap of debris down which the great owl had charged at me, I found the last low chamber, the place I was seeking. And there in a pile of sticks lay an egg, an impressive egg, glimmering palely in the cavernous gloom, full of potentialities, and fraught, if I may say so, with destiny.

I affected at first to ignore it. I was after the buried treasures that lay beneath its nest in the cave floor. The egg was simply going to have to look after itself. Its parent had gone, and in a pretty rude fashion, too. I was no vandal, but I was going to be firm. If an owl's egg stood in the path of science— But suddenly the egg seemed very helpless, very much alone. I probed in the earth around the nest. The nest got in the way. This was a time for decision.

I know a primatologist who will lift a rifle and shoot a baby monkey out of its mother's arms for the sake of science. He is a good man, too, and goes home nights to his wife. I tried to focus on this thought as I faced the egg.

I knew it was a rare egg. The race of its great and

lonely mother was growing scant in these mountains and would soon be gone. Under it might lie a treasure that would make me famed in the capitals of science, but suppose there was nothing under the nest after all and I destroyed it? Suppose . . .

Here in this high, sterile silence with the wind crying over frightful precipices, myself and that egg were the only living things. That seemed to me to mean something. At last and quietly I backed out of the cave and slipped down into the chasm out of which I had come. By luck I did not fall.

Sometimes in these later years I think perhaps the skull was there, the skull that could have made me famous. It is not so bad, however, when I think that the egg became an owl. I had had charge of it in the universe's sight for a single hour, and I had done well by life.

It is not the loss of the skull that torments me sometimes on winter evenings. Suppose the big, unutterably frightened bird never came back to its egg? A feeling of vast loss and desolation sweeps over me then. I begin to perceive what it is to doubt.

IV

It was years later that I met the old man. He was waiting in my office when I came in. It was obvious from the timid glances of my secretary that he had been passed from hand to hand and that he had outwitted everybody. Someone in the background made a twisting motion at his forehead.

The old man sat, a colossal ruin, in the reception chair. The squirrel-like twitterings of the office people did not disturb him.

As I came forward he fished in a ragged wallet and produced a clipping. "You made this speech?" he asked.

"Why, yes," I said.

"You said men came here late? A few thousand years ago?"

"Yes, you see—"

"Young man," he interrupted, "you are frightfully wrong."

I was aware that his eyes were contracted to pin points and seemed in some danger of protruding on stalks.

"You have ignored," he rumbled, "the matter of the Miocene period—the Golden Age. A great civilization existed then, far more splendid than this—degenerate time." He struck the floor fiercely with his cane.

"But," I protested, "that period is twenty million years ago. Man wasn't even in existence. Geology shows—"

"Nothing!" said the massive relic. "Geology has nothing to do with it. Sit down. I know all about the Golden Age. I will prove to you that you are wrong."

I collapsed doubtfully into a chair. He told me that he was from some little town in Missouri, but I never believed it for a moment. He smelled bad, and it was obvious that if he brought news of the Golden Age, as he claimed, he had come by devious and dreadful ways from that far era.

"I have here," he said, thrusting his head forward and breathing heavily into my face, "a human jaw. I will unwrap it a little and you can see. It is from a cave I found."

"It is embedded in stalactite drippings," I murmured, hypnotized against my will. "That might represent considerable age. Where did you find it?"

He raised a protesting hand. "Later, son, later. You admit then—?"

I strained forward. "Those teeth," I said, "they are large —they look primitive." The feeling I had had at the mouth of the owl's cave came to me again overpoweringly. "Let me see a little more of the jaw. If the mental eminence should be lacking, you may have something important. Just let me handle it a moment."

With the scuttling alacrity of a crab, the old man drew back and popped the papers over his find. "You admit, then, that it is important? That it proves the Golden Age was real?"

Baffled, I looked at him. He eyed me with an equal wariness.

"Where did you find it?" I asked. "In this light it seemed—it might be—a fossil man. We have been looking a long time. If you would only let me see—"

"I found it in a cave in Missouri," he droned in a rote fashion. "You can never find the cave alone. If you will make a statement to the papers that the Golden Age is true, I will go with you. You have seen the evidence."

Once more I started to protest. "But this has nothing to do with the Golden Age. You may have a rare human fossil there. You are denying science—"

"Science," said the old man with frightening dignity, "is illusion." He arose. "I will not come back. You must make a choice."

For one long moment we looked at each other across the fantastic barriers of our individual minds. Then, on his heavy oakwood cane, he hobbled to the door and was gone. I watched through the window as he crossed the street in a patch of autumn sunlight as phantasmal and unreal as he. Leaves fell raggedly around him until, a tatter among tatters, he passed from sight.

I rubbed a hand over my eyes, and it seemed the secretary looked at me strangely. How was it that I had failed this time? By unbelief? But the man was mad. I could not possibly have made such a statement as he wanted.

Was it pride that cost me that strange jaw bone? Was it academic dignity? Should I have followed him? Found where he lived? Importuned his relatives? Stolen if necessary, that remarkable fragment?

Of course I should! I know that now. Of course I should.

Thirty years have passed since the old man came to see me. I have crawled in many caverns, stooped with infinite aching patience over the bones of many men. I have made no great discoveries.

I think now that in some strange way that old man out of the autumn leaf-fall was the last test of the inscrutable gods. There will be no further chances. The egg and the spiders and the madman—in them is the obituary of a life dedicated to the folly of doubt, the life of a small bone hunter.

13

THE MIND AS NATURE

WHEN I was a small boy I lived, more than most children, in two worlds. One was dark, hidden, and self-examining, though in its own way not without compensations. The other world in which I somehow also managed to exist was external, boisterous, and what I suppose the average parent would call normal or extroverted. These two worlds simultaneously existing in one growing brain had in them something of the dichotomy present in the actual universe, where one finds, behind the ridiculous, wonderful tent show of woodpeckers, giraffes, and hoptoads, some kind of dark, brooding, but creative void out of which these things emerge—some antimatter universe, some web of dark tensions running beneath and creating the superficial show of form that so delights us. If I develop this little story of a personal experience as a kind of parable, it is because I believe that in one way or another we mirror in ourselves the universe with all its dark vacuity and also its simultaneous urge to create anew, in each generation, the beauty and the terror of our mortal existence.

In my own case, through the accidents of fortune, the disparity between these two worlds was vastly heightened. How I managed to exist in both I do not know. Children under such disharmony often grow sick, retire inward, choose to return to the void. I have known such cases. I am not unaware that I paid a certain price for my survival and indeed have been paying for it ever since. Yet the curious thing is that I survived and, looking back, I have a growing feeling that the experience was good for me. I think I learned something from it even while I passed through certain humiliations and an utter and profound loneliness. I was living in a primitive world at the same time that I was inhabiting the modern world as it existed in the second decade of this century. I am not talking now about the tree-house, cave-building activities of normal boys. I am talking about the minds of the first dawning human consciousness—about a kind of mental ice age, and of how a light came in from outside until as I have indicated, two worlds existed in which a boy, still a single unsplit personality, walked readily from one world to the other by day and by night without anyone observing the invisible boundaries he passed.

I

To begin this story I have to strip myself of certain conventions, but since all the major figures of my childhood are dead I can harm no one but myself. I think, if we are to find our way into the nature of creativeness, into those multitudinous universes that inhabit the minds of men, such case histories—though I hate this demeaning term—have a certain value. Perhaps if we were franker on these matters, we might reach out and occasionally touch, with a passing radiance, some other star in the night.

I was born in the first decade of this century, conceived in and part of the rolling yellow cloud that occasionally raises up a rainy silver eye to look upon itself before subsiding into dust again. That cloud has been blowing in my part of the Middle West since the ice age. Only a few months ago, flying across the continent, I knew we were passing over it in its customary place. It was still there and its taste was still upon my tongue.

In those days I lived, like most American boys of that section, in a small house where the uncemented cellar occasionally filled with water and the parlor was kept shuttered in a perpetual cool darkness. We never had visitors. No minister ever called on us, so the curtains were never raised. We were, in a sense, social outcasts. We were not bad people nor did we belong to a racial minority. We were simply shunned as unimportant and odd.

The neighbors were justified in this view. As I have mentioned, my mother was stone-deaf; my father worked the long hours of a time when labor was still labor. I was growing up alone in a house whose dead silence was broken only by the harsh discordant jangling of a voice that could not hear itself. My mother had lost her hearing as a young girl. I never learned what had attracted my father to her. I never learned by what fantastic chance I had come to exist at all. Only the cloud would know, I sometimes think to this day, only the yellow loess cloud rolling, impenetrable as it was when our ancestors first emerged from it on the ice-age steppes of Europe, or when they followed the bison into its heart on the wide American plains.

I turned over the bricks of our front sidewalk and watched ants with a vague interest. There grew up between my mother and myself an improvised system of communication, consisting of hand signals, stampings on the floor to create vibrations, exaggerated lip movements vaguely reminiscent of an anthropoid society. We did not consciously work at this; we were far too ignorant. Certain acts were merely found useful and came to be repeated and to take on symbolic value. It was something of the kind of communication which may have been conducted by the man-apes of the early ice age. One might say we were at the speech threshold—not much more.

I did not go to church, and since the family was not agreed upon any mode of worship, I merely wondered as I grew older how it was that things came to be. In short, I would have been diagnosed today by social workers as a person suffering from societal deprivation and headed for trouble.

There was another curious aspect of this family which involved my father. He was a good man who bore the asperities of my afflicted mother with dignity and restraint. He had been a strolling intinerant actor in his younger years, a largely self-trained member of one of those little troupes who played *East Lynne* and declaimed raw Shakespearean melodrama to unsophisticated audiences in the little Midwestern "opera houses." He had a beautiful resonant speaking voice. Although we owned no books, and although when I knew him in middle age a harsh life had dimmed every hunger except that for rest, he could still declaim long rolling Elizabethan passages that caused shivers to run up my back.

> "Give me my Robe, put on my Crowne; I have
> Immortall longings in me."

Like many failures of his time he used to speak wistfully of cheap land in Arkansas and send for catalogues, searching for something that was permanently lost. It was the last of the dream that had finally perished under the yellow cloud. I use the word "failure" in a worldly sense only. He was not a failure as a man. He reared a son, the product of an unfortunate marriage from which he might easily have fled, leaving me inarticulate. He was kind and thoughtful with an innate courtesy that no school in that rough land had taught him. Although he was intensely sensitive, I saw him weep but twice. The first time, when I was young and very ill, I looked up in astonishment as a tear splashed on my hand. The second time, long years afterward, belongs to him and his life alone. I will merely say he had had a great genius for love and that his luck was very bad. He was not fitted for life under the yellow cloud. He knew it, yet played out his role there to the end. So poor were we, it took me twenty years to put a monument upon his grave.

II

We come now to the two worlds of which I spoke, the two worlds making up the mind and heart of this curiously deprived and solitary child—a child whose mother's speech was negligible and disordered and which left him for the greater part of his early childhood involved with only rudimentary communication and the conscious rebuffs of neighbors, or another ill-understood world of haunting grandiloquent words at which his playmates laughed; or even a third world where he sat, the last little boy allowed in the street, and watched the green night moths beat past under the street lamps.

Into what well of being does one then descend for strength? How does one choose one's life? Or does one just go on without guidance, as in the dark town of my youth, from one spot of light to the next? "Uncertainty," as John Dewey has well said, "is primarily a practical matter. It signifies uncertainty of the *issue* of present experiences.

These are fraught with future peril. . . . The intrinsic troublesome and uncertain quality of situations lies in the fact that they hold outcomes in suspense; they move to evil or to good fortune. The natural tendency of man is to do something at once, there is impatience with suspense, and lust for immediate action."

It is here, amid a chaos of complexities, that the teacher, frequently with blindness, with uncertainties of his own, must fight with circumstance for the developing mind—perhaps even for the very survival of the child. The issue cannot be long delayed, because, as Dewey observes, man—and far more, the child—has a lust for the immediate, for action. Yet the teacher is fighting for an oncoming future, for something that has not emerged, which may, in fact, never emerge. His lot is worse than that of the sculptors in snow, which Sydney Hook once described us as being. Rather, the teacher is a sculptor of the intangible future. There is no more dangerous occupation on the planet, for what we conceive as our masterpiece may appear out of time to mock us—a horrible caricature of ourselves.

The teacher must ever walk warily between the necessity of inducing those conformities which in every generation reaffirm our rebellious humanity, and of allowing for the free play of the creative spirit. It is not only for the sake of the future that the true educator fights, it is for the justification of himself, his profession, and the state of his own soul. He, too, amid contingencies and weariness, without mental antennae, and with tests that fail him, is a savior of souls. He is giving shapes to time, and the shapes themselves, driven by their own inner violence, wrench free of his control—must, if they are truly sculptured, surge like released genii from the classroom, or tragically shrink to something less than bottle size.

The teacher cannot create, any more than can the sculptor, the stone upon which he exercises his talents; he cannot, it is true, promote gene changes and substitutions in the bodies with which he works. But here again Dewey has words of peculiar pertinence to us—words which remove from the genes something of the utter determinacy in which the geneticist sometimes revels. "In the continuous ongoing of life," he contends, "objects part with something of their final character and become conditions of subsequent experiences. There is regulation of the change in which . . . a causal character is rendered preparatory and instrumental."

The boy under the street lamp may become fascinated by night-flying moths or the delinquent whisperings of companions. Or he may lie awake in the moonlight of his room, quaking with the insecurity of a divided household and the terrors of approaching adulthood. He may quietly continue some lost part of childhood by playing gentle and abstract games with toys he would not dare to introduce among his raucous companions of the street. He wanders forlornly through a museum and is impressed by a kindly scientist engrossed in studying some huge bones.

Objects do indeed "part with something of their final character," and so do those who teach. There are subjects in which I have remained dwarfed all of my adult life because of the ill-considered blow of someone nursing pent-up aggressions, or because of words more violent in their end effects than blows. There are other subjects for which I have more than ordinary affection because they are associated in my mind with kindly and understanding men or women—sculptors who left even upon such impliant clay as mine the delicate chiseling of refined genius, who gave unwittingly something of their final character to most unpromising material. Sculptors reaching blindly forward into time, they struck out their creation, scarce living to view the result.

Now, for many years an educator, I often feel the need to seek out a quiet park bench to survey mentally that vast and nameless river of students which has poured under my hands. In pain I have meditated: "This man is dead—a suicide. Was it I, all unknowingly, who directed, in some black hour, his hand upon the gun? This man is a liar and a cheat. Where did my stroke go wrong?" Or there comes to memory the man who, after long endeavors, returned happily to the farm from which he had come. Did I serve him, if not in the world's eye, well? Or the richly endowed young poet whom I sheltered from his father's wrath—was I pampering or defending—and at the right or the wrong moment in his life? Contingency, contingency, and each day by word or deed the chisel falling true or blind upon the future of some boy or girl.

Ours is an ill-paid profession and we have our share of fools. We, too, like the generation before us, are the cracked, the battered, the malformed products of remoter chisels shaping the most obstinate substance in the universe—the substance of man. Someone has to do it, but perhaps it might be done more kindly, more precisely, to the extent that we are consciously aware of what we do—even if that thought sometimes congeals our hearts with terror. Or, if we were more conscious of our task, would our hands shake or grow immobilized upon the chisel?

I do not know. I know only that in these late faint-hearted years I sometimes pause with my hand upon the knob before I go forth into the classroom. I am afflicted in this fashion because I have come to follow Dewey in his statement that "nature is seen to be marked by histories." As an evolutionist I am familiar with that vast sprawling emergent, the universe, and its even more fantastic shadow, life. Stranger still, however, is the record of the artist who creates the symbols by which we live. As Dewey has again anticipated, "No mechanically exact science of an individual is possible. An individual is a history unique in character. But"—he adds—"constituents of an individual are known when they are regarded not as qualitative, but as statistical constants derived from a series of operations."

I should like to survey briefly a few such constants from the lives of certain great literary figures with whose works I happen to be reasonably familiar. I choose to do so because creativity—that enigma to which the modern student of educational psychology is devoting more and more attention—is particularly "set in the invisible." "The tangible," Dewey insisted in *Experience and Nature*, "rests precariously upon the untouched and ungrasped." Dewey abhorred the inculcation of fixed conclusions at the expense of man's originality. Though my case histories are neither numerous nor similar, they contain certain constants which, without revealing the total nature of genius, throw light upon the odd landscapes and interiors that have nurtured it.

III

"A person too early cut off from the common interests of men," Jean Rostand, the French biologist, once remarked, "is exposed to inner impoverishment. Like those islands which are lacking in some whole class of mammals." Naturally there are degrees of such isolation, but I would venture the observation that this eminent observer has overlooked one thing: sometimes on such desert islands there has been a great evolutionary proliferation amongst the flora and fauna that remain. Strange shapes, exotic growths, which, on the mainland, would have been quickly strangled by formidable enemies, here spring up readily. Sometimes the rare, the beautiful, can only emerge or survive in isolation. In a similar manner, some degree of withdrawal serves to nurture man's creative powers. The artist and the scientist bring out of the dark void, like the mysterious universe itself, the unique, the strange, the unexpected. Numerous observers have testified upon the loneliness of the process.

"The whole of my pleasure," wrote Charles Darwin of his travels with illiterate companions on the high Andean uplands, "was derived from what passed in my mind." The mind, in other words, has a latent, lurking fertility, not unrelated to the universe from which it sprang. Even in want and in jail it will labor, and if it does not produce a physical escape, it will appear, assuming the motivational drive to be great enough, in *Pilgrim's Progress*, that still enormously moving account of one who walked through the wilderness of this world and laid him down and dreamed a dream. That dream, as John Bunyan himself wrote, "will make a Traveller of Thee." It was the account of the journey from the City of Destruction to the City of God. It was written by a man in homespun not even aware of being a conscious artist, not interested in personal fame. Three centuries later he is better known than many kings.

The fact is that many of us who walk to and fro upon our usual tasks are prisoners drawing mental maps of escape. I once knew a brilliant and discerning philosopher who spent many hours each week alone in movie houses, watching indifferently pictures of a quality far below his actual intellectual tastes. I knew him as an able, friendly, and normal person. Somewhere behind this sunny mask, however, he was in flight, from what, I never knew. Was it job, home, family—or was it rather something lost that he was seeking? Whatever it was, the pictures that passed before his eyes, the sounds, only half-heard, could have meant little except for an occasional face, a voice, a fading bar of music. The darkness and the isolation were what he wanted, something in the deep night of himself that called him home.

The silver screen was only a doorway to a land he had entered long ago. It was weirdly like hashish or opium. He taught well; he was far better read than many who climbed to national reputation upon fewer abilities than he possessed. His kindness to others was proverbial, his advice the sanest a friend could give. Only the pen was denied to him and so he passed toward his end, leaving behind the quick streak of a falling star that slips from sight. A genius in personal relationships, he was voiceless— somewhere a door had been softly, courteously, but inexorably closed within his brain. It would never open again within his lifetime.

I knew another man of similar capacities—a scholar who had shifted in his last graduate days from the field of the classics to the intricacies of zoology. A scintillating piece of research had rocked his profession, and he had marched steadily to the leadership of a great department. He was a graying, handsome man, with the world at his feet. He did not fail in health; his students loved him, and he loved them. The research died. This happens to other men. His problem was more serious: he could not answer letters. His best pupils could not depend upon him even to recommend them for posts or scholarships. Airmail letters lay unopened in his box. It was not that he was cruel. Anything a man could do by word of mouth he would do for his students, even the assumption of unpleasant tasks. Firm, upright, with a grave old-fashioned gallantry, in him also a door had closed forever. One never heard him speak of his family. Somewhere behind that door was a landscape we were never permitted to enter.

One can also read case histories. There is, for example, the brilliant child who had lost a parent and then a guardian abroad. Here, in some strange transmutation, arose a keen cartographer, a map maker, seeking a way back to the lost—a student of continents, time tables, odd towns, and fading roads. This is a juvenile case and the end therefore uncertain. One wonders whether there will come a breaking point where, as eventually they must, the trails within dissolve to waving grass and the crossroad signs lie twisted and askew on rotting posts. Where, then, will the wanderer turn? Will the last sign guide him safely home at last—or will he become one of the dawdlers, the evaders, unconscious fighters of some cruel inner master? It is of great interest in this connection that Herman Melville, who had lost his father under painful circumstances in his youth, describes in *Redburn*, in fictional guise, what must have lain close to his own heart: the following of a thirty-year-old map which traced the wanderings of Redburn's father in Liverpool. These passages are handled with the kind of imaginative power that indicates Melville's deep personal involvement in this aspect of Redburn's story. He speaks of running in the hope of overtaking the lost father at the next street; then the map fails him, just as the father himself had gone where no son's search could find him. Again in *Moby Dick* he cries out, "Where is the foundling's father hidden?" I think of my own slow journey homeward along those arc lights in a city whose name now comes with difficulty to my tongue.

In some of us a child—lost, strayed off the beaten path —goes wandering to the end of time while we, in another garb, grow up, marry or seduce, have children, hold jobs, or sit in movies, and refuse to answer our mail. Or, by contrast, we haunt our mailboxes, impelled by some strange anticipation of a message that will never come. "A man," Thoreau has commented, "needs only to be turned around once with his eyes shut in this world to be lost."

But now an odd thing happens. Some of the men with maps in their heads do not remain mute. Instead, they develop the power to draw the outside world within and lose us there. Or, as scientists, after some deep inner colloquy, they venture even to remake reality.

What would the modern chronicler of the lives of Hollywood celebrities feel if he were told he had to produce a great autobiography out of a year spent in a shack by a little pond, seeing scarcely anyone? Yet Thoreau did just that, and in entering what was essentially an inner forest, he influenced the lives of thousands of people all over the world and, it would appear, through succeeding generations.

There was another man, Nathaniel Hawthorne, who, as he put it, "sat down by the wayside of life, like a man under enchantment." For over a decade he wrote in a room in Salem, subsisting on a small income, and scarcely going out before evening. "I am surrounding myself with shadows," he wrote, "which bewilder me by aping the realities of life." He found in the human heart "a terrible gloom, and monsters of diverse kinds . . . but deeper still . . . the eternal beauty." This region of guttering candles, ungainly night birds, "fragments of a world," are an interior geography through which even the modern callous reader ventures with awe.

One could run through other great creative landscapes in the literary field. One could move with Hudson over the vast Patagonian landscape which haunted him even in his long English exile. One could, in fact, devise an anthology in which, out of the same natural background, under the same stars, beneath the same forests, or upon the same seas, each man would evoke such smoky figures from his own heart, such individual sunlight and shadow as would be his alone. Antoine de St.-Exupéry had his own flyer's vision of the little South American towns, or of the Andes, when flying was still young. Or Herman Melville, whose Pacific was "a Potters Field of all four continents . . . mixed shades and shadows, drowned dreams, somnambulisms, reveries."

Or, to change scene into the city-world, there is the vision of London in Arthur Machen's *Hill of Dreams*: "one grey temple of an awful rite, ring within ring of wizard stones circled about some central place, every circle was an initiation, every initiation eternal loss." Perhaps it should not go unnoticed that in this tale of solitude in a great city Machen dwells upon the hatred of the average man for the artist, "a deep instinctive dread of all that was strange, uncanny, alien to his nature." Julian, Machen's hero, "could not gain the art of letters and he had lost the art of humanity." He was turning fatally inward as surely as those men whose stories I have recounted.

Perhaps there is a moral here which should not go unobserved, and which makes the artist's problem greater. It also extends to the scientist, particularly as in the case of Darwin or Freud, or, in earlier centuries, such men as Giordano Bruno or Francis Bacon. "Humanity is not, as was once thought," says John Dewey, "the end for which all things were formed; it is but a slight and feeble thing, perhaps an episodic one, in the vast stretch of the universe. But for man, man is the center of interest and the measure of importance."

IV

It is frequently the tragedy of the great artist, as it is of the great scientist, that he frightens the ordinary man. If he is more than a popular story-teller it may take humanity a generation to absorb and grow accustomed to the new geography with which the scientist or artist presents us. Even then, perhaps only the more imaginative and literate may accept him. Subconsciously the genius is feared as an image breaker; frequently he does not accept the opinions of the mass, or man's opinion of himself. He has voiced through the ages, in one form or another, this very loneliness and detachment which Dewey saw so clearly at the outcome of our extending knowledge. The custombound, uneducated, intolerant man projects his fear and hatred upon the seer. The artist is frequently a human mirror. If what we see there displeases us, if we see all too clearly our own insignificance and vanity, we tend to revolt, not against ourselves, but in order to martyrize the unfortunate soul who forced us into self-examination.

In short, like the herd animals we are, we sniff warily at the strange one among us. If he is fortunate enough finally to be accepted, it is likely to be after a trial of ridicule and after the sting has been removed from his work by long familiarization and bowdlerizing, when the alien quality of his thought has been mitigated or removed. Carl Schneer recounts that Einstein made so little impression on his superiors, it was with difficulty that he obtained even a junior clerkship in the Swiss Patents office at Bern, after having failed of consideration as a scholar of promise. Not surprisingly, theoretical physicists favored his views before the experimentalists capitulated. As Schneer remarks: "It was not easy to have a twenty-six-year-old clerk in the Swiss Patents office explain the meaning of experiments on which one had labored for years." Implacable hatred, as well as praise, was to be Einstein's lot.

To an anthropologist, the social reception of invention reminds one of the manner in which a strange young male is first repulsed, then tolerated, upon the fringes of a group of howler monkeys he wishes to join. Finally, since the memories of the animals are short, he becomes familiar, is accepted, and fades into the mass. In a similar way, discoveries made by Darwin and Wallace were at first castigated and then by degrees absorbed. In the process both men experienced forms of loneliness and isolation, not simply as a necessity for discovery but as a penalty for having dared to redraw the map of our outer, rather than inner, cosmos.

This fear of the upheld mirror in the hand of genius extends to the teaching profession and perhaps to the primary and secondary school teacher most of all. The teacher occupies, as we shall see a little further on, a particularly anomalous and exposed position in a society subject to rapid change or threatened by exterior enemies.

Society is never totally sure of what it wants of its educators. It wants, first of all, the inculcation of custom, tradition, and all that socializes the child into the good citizen. In the lower grades the demand for conformity is likely to be intense. The child himself, as well as the teacher, is frequently under the surveillance of critical, if not opinionated, parents. Secondly, however, society wants the child to absorb new learning which will simultaneously benefit that society and enhance the individual's prospects of success.

Thus the teacher, in some degree, stands as interpreter and disseminator of the cultural mutations introduced by the individual genius into society. Some of the fear, the projected guilt feelings, of those who do not wish to look into the mirrors held up to them by men of the Hawthorne stamp of genius, falls upon us. Moving among innovators of ideas as we do, sifting and judging them daily, something of the suspicion with which the mass of mankind still tends to regard its own cultural creators falls upon the teacher who plays a role of great significance in this process of cultural diffusion. He is, to a degree, placed in a paradoxical position. He is expected both to be the guardian of stability and the exponent of societal change. Since all persons do not accept new ideas at the same rate, it is impossible for the educator to please the entire society even if he remains abjectly servile. This is particularly true in a dynamic and rapidly changing era like the present.

Moreover, the true teacher has another allegiance than that to parents alone. More than any other class in society, teachers mold the future in the minds of the young. They transmit to them the aspirations of great thinkers of which their parents may have only the faintest notions. The teacher is often the first to discover the talented and unusual scholar. How he handles and encourages, or discourages, such a child may make all the difference in the world to that child's future—and to the world. Perhaps he can induce in stubborn parents the conviction that their child is unusual and should be encouraged in his studies. If the teacher is sufficiently judicious, he may even be able to help a child over the teetering planks of a broken home and a bad neighborhood. Like a responsible doctor, he knows that he will fail in many instances—that circumstances will destroy, or genes prove defective beyond hope. There is a limit, furthermore, to the energy of one particular man or woman in dealing individually with a growing mass of students.

It is just here, however—in our search for what we might call the able, all-purpose, success-modeled student —that I feel it so necessary not to lose sight of those darker, more uncertain, late-maturing, sometimes painfully abstracted youths who may represent the Darwins, Thoreaus, and Hawthornes of the next generation. As Dr. Carroll Newsom emphasized in his admirable book, *A University President Speaks Out*: real college education is not a four-year process; it should be lifelong. Men, moreover, mature in many ways and fashions. It is uncertain what Darwin's or Wallace's chances of passing a modern college board examination might have been.

I believe it useful, and not demeaning to the teaching profession, to remember Melville's words in 1850, at a time when he was fighting horribly with the materials of what was to become his greatest book. The words, besides being prophetic in his case, bespeak the philosopher who looks beyond man as he is. He said: "I somehow cling to the wondrous fancy, that in all men hiddenly reside certain wondrous, occult properties—as in some plants and minerals—which by some happy but very rare accident . . . may chance to be called forth here on earth."

As a teacher I know little about how these remarkable events come about, but I have seen them happen. I believe in them. I believe they are more likely to happen late in those whose background has been one of long dep-

rivation. I believe that the good teacher should never grow
indifferent to their possibility—not, at least, if there is evidence, even in the face of failure in some subjects, of high
motivation and intelligence in some specific field.

At the height of his creative powers, Thoreau wrote that
"we should treat our minds as innocent and ingenuous
children whose guardians we are—be careful what objects
and what subjects we thrust on their attention. Even the
facts of science may dust the mind by their dryness, unless
they are in a sense effaced each morning, or rather rendered fertile by the dews of fresh and living truth. Every
thought that passes through the mind helps to wear and
tear it, and to deepen the ruts, which, as in the streets of
Pompeii, evince how much it has been used. How many
things there are concerning which we might well deliber-
ate whether we had better know them!"

V

Educators responsible to society will appreciate that
certain of these ancient institutions by which men live are,
however involved with human imperfection, the supporting bones of the societal body. Without them, without a
certain degree of conformity and habit, society would literally cease to exist. The problem lies in sustaining the airy
flight of the superior intellect above the necessary ruts it is
forced to travel. As Thoreau comments, the heel of the
true author wears out no road. "A thinker's weight is in his
thought, not in his tread."

A direct analogy is evident in the biological domain,
where uncontrolled diversification at the species level
would make for maladaptation to the environment. Yet
without the emergence of superior or differently adapted
individuals—beneficial mutations, in other words—the
doorways to prolonged survival of the species would,

under changing conditions, be closed. Similarly, if society sinks into the absolute rut of custom, if it refuses to accept beneficial mutations in the cultural realm or to tolerate, if not promote, the life of genius, then its unwieldy slumbers may be its last. Worse is the fact that all we know of beauty and the delights of free untrammeled thought may sink to a few concealed sparks glimmering warily behind the foreheads of men no longer in a position to transfer these miraculous mutations to the society which gave them birth.

Such repression is equivalent to placing an animal with a remarkable genetic heritage alone on a desert island. His strain will perish without issue. And so it is, in analogous ways, in oppressive societies or even in societies not consciously oppressive. It is all too easy to exist in an atmosphere of supposed free speech and yet bring such pressures upon the individual that he is afraid to speak openly. I do not refer to political matters alone. There was a time in the American world when Thoreau's advice to "catalogue stars, those thoughts whose orbits are as rarely calculated as comets" could be set down without undergoing the scrutiny of twenty editors or publishers' readers. The observer of the fields was free as the astronomer to watch the aspect of his own interior heavens. He could even say boldly that he was "not concerned to express that kind of truth which Nature has expressed. Who knows but I may suggest some things to her?"

Our faith in science has become so great that, though the open-ended and novelty-producing aspect of nature is scientifically recognized in the physics and biology of our time, there is often a reluctance to give voice to it in other than professional jargon. It has been my own experience among students, laymen, and scholars that to express even wonder about the universe—in other words, to benefit from some humble consideration of what we do not know, as well as marching to the constant drum-beat of what we call the age of technology—is regarded askance in some quarters. I have had the vague word "mystic" applied to me because I have not been able to shut out wonder occasionally, when I have looked at the world. I have been lectured by at least one member of my profession who advised me to "explain myself"—words which sound for all the world like a humorless request for the self-accusations so popular in Communist lands. Although I have never disturbed the journals in my field with my off-hour compositions, there seemed to be a feeling on the part of this eminent colleague that something vaguely heretical about the state of my interior heavens demanded exposure or "confession" in a scientific journal. This man was unaware, in his tough laboratory attitude, that there was another world of pure reverie that is of at least equal importance to the human soul. Ironically, only a decade ago Robert Hofstadter, Nobel Prize winner in physics, revealed a humility which would greatly become the lesser men of our age. "Man," he said wistfully, "will never find the end of the trail."

VI

Directly stated, the evolution of the entire universe— stars, elements, life, man—is a process of drawing something out of nothing, out of the utter void of nonbeing. The creative element in the mind of man—that latency which can conceive gods, carve statues, move the heart with the symbols of great poetry, or devise the formulas of modern physics—emerges in as mysterious a fashion as those elementary particles which leap into momentary existence in great cyclotrons, only to vanish again like infinitesimal ghosts. The reality we know in our limited lifetimes is dwarfed by the unseen potential of the abyss where science stops. In a similar way the smaller universe of the individual human brain has its lonely cometary passages or flares suddenly like a supernova, only to subside in death while the waves of energy it has released roll on through unnumbered generations.

As the astrophysicist gazes upon the rare releases of power capable of devastating an entire solar system, so does the student of the behavioral sciences wonder at the manifestations of creative genius and consider whether the dark mechanisms that control the doorways of the human mind might be tripped open at more frequent intervals. Does genius emerge from the genes alone? Does the largely unknown chemistry of the brain contain at least part of the secret? Or is the number of potential cell connections involved? Or do we ordinary men carry it irretrievably locked within our subconscious minds?

That the *manifestations* of genius are culturally controlled we are well aware. The urban world, in all its diversity, provides a background, a cultural base, without which—whatever may be hidden in great minds—creativity would have had to seek other and more ephemeral expression or remain mute. Yet no development in art or scientific theory from the upper Stone Age onward seems to have demanded any further development in the brain of man. Mathematical theory, science, the glories of art lurked hidden as the potential seeds of the universe itself, in the minds of children rocked to sleep by cave fires in ice-age Europe.

If genius is a purely biological phenomenon one must assume that the chances of its appearance should increase with the size of populations. Yet it is plain that, as with toadstools which spring up in the night in fairy rings and then vanish, there is some delicate soil which nurtures genius—the cultural circumstance and the play of minds must meet. It is not a matter of population statistics alone, else there would not have been so surprising an efflorescence of genius in fifth-century Greece—a thing we still marvel at in our vastly expanded world. Darwin, committed to biological explanations alone, was left fumbling uncertainly with a problem that was essentially not reducible to a simplistic biological explanation. Without ignoring the importance of biology as one aspect of an infinitely complicated subject, therefore, the modern researcher favors the view that the intensive examination of the creative mind and its environment may offer some hope of stimulating the sources from which it springs, or, at the very least, of nurturing it more carefully.

I have touched upon loneliness, the dweller in the forest as represented by Thoreau, the isolated man in the room who was Hawthorne, and such wandering recluse scientists as Darwin and Wallace. This loneliness, in the case of literary men, frequently leads to an intense self-examination. "Who placed us with eyes between a microscopic and telescopic world?" questions Thoreau. "I have the habit of attention to such excess that my senses get no rest, but suffer from a constant strain."

Thoreau here expresses the intense self-awareness which is both the burden and delight of the true artist. It is not merely the fact that such men create their universe as surely as shipwrecked bits of life run riot and transform themselves on oceanic islands. It is that in this supremely heightened consciousness of genius the mind insists on expression. The spirit literally cannot remain within itself. It will talk if it talks on paper only to itself, as did Thoreau.

Anxiety, the disease which many psychiatrists seek to excise completely from the human psyche, is here carried to painful but enormously creative heights. The freedom of genius, its passage beyond the bonds of culture which control the behavior of the average man, in itself demands the creation of new modes of being. William Butler Yeats comments with penetration:

> "Man's life is thought and he despite his terror
>   cannot cease
> Ravening through century after century . . .
> That he may come
> Into the desolation of reality."

Within that desolation, whether he be scientist or poet, man—for this is the nature of his inmost being—will build ever anew. It is not in his nature to do otherwise.

Thoreau, however, presents in his writing an interesting paradox. In his reference to the excessive strain of heightened attention, one might get the impression that creativity was to him a highly conscious exercise that had wriggled into his very fingertips. That he was an intensely perceptive observer there can be no question. Yet he wrote, in those pre-Freudian, pre-Jungian days of 1852:

"I catch myself philosophizing most abstractly when first returning to consciousness in the night or morning. I make the truest observations and distinctions then, when the will is yet wholly asleep and the mind works like a machine without friction. I am conscious of having, in my sleep, transcended the limits of the individual, and made observations and carried on conversations which in my waking hours I can neither recall nor appreciate. As if in sleep our individual fell into the infinite mind, and at the moment of awakening we found ourselves on the confines of the latter."

"It is," he confides in another place, "the material of all things loose and set afloat that makes my sea."

The psychiatrist Lawrence Kubie has speculated that "the creative person is one who in some manner, which today is still accidental, has retained his capacity to use his pre-conscious functions more freely than is true of others who may potentially be equally gifted." While I do not believe that the time will ever come when each man can release his own Shakespeare, I do not doubt that the freedom to create is somehow linked with facility of access to those obscure regions below the conscious mind.

There is, perhaps, a wonderful analogy here between the potential fecundity of life in the universe and those novelties which natural selection in a given era permits to break through the living screen, the biosphere, into reality. Organic opportunity has thus placed sharp limits upon a far greater life potential than is ever permitted to enter the actual world. This other hidden world, a world of possible but nonexistent futures, is a constant accompaniment, a real but wholly latent twin, of the nature in which we have our being. In a strangely similar manner the mental censor of a too rigidly blocked or distorted unconscious may interfere, not alone with genius, but even with what might be called ordinary productivity.

Just as, in a given situation, the living biological screen may prevent the emergence of a higher form of life or precipitate its destruction, so in that dark, soundless area of the brain, which parallels the similarly pregnant void of space, much may be barred from creation that exists only as a potentiality. Here again, culturally imposed forms and individual experiences may open or keep permanently closed the doorways of life. The role of purely genetic expression becomes frightfully obscured by the environmental complexities which surround the birth and development of the individual. There is no doubt that clinical studies devoted to creativity, including private interviews with cooperating and contemporary men of genius, offer the prospect of gaining greater insight into those dark alleys and byways out of which stumble at infrequent intervals the Shelleys, the Shakespeares, the Newtons, and the Darwins of our world.

Sometimes they are starved by poverty, sometimes self-schooled, sometimes they have known wealth, sometimes they have appeared like comets across an age of violence.

Or they have been selfless, they have been beautiful or unlovely of body, they have been rake or puritan. One thing
alone they have had in common: thought, music, art,
transmissible but unique.

VII

If we, as ordinary educators, have the task which
Dewey envisioned of transmitting from these enrichers of
life their wisdom to the unformed turbulent future, of
transforming reflection into action consonant with their
thought, then some of their luminosity must encompass
our minds; their passion must, in some degree, break
through our opaque thoughts and descend to us. Whether
we will it so or not, we play, in another form, the part of
the biological screen in the natural world, or the psychological censor to the individual human mind.

As educators, we play this role in our own culture. In
innumerable small ways, if we are rigid, dogmatic, arro-
gant, we shall be laying stone upon stone, an ugly thing.
We shall, for such is our power, give the semblance of
necessary reality to a future that need never have been
permitted. The educator can be the withholder as well as
the giver of life.

I began by offering a case history for examination, the
case history of an obscure educator who, within the course
of a single lifetime, has passed from a world of almost primordial illiteracy and isolation to one which permits wandering at will among such towering minds as I have been
discussing. In the end, their loneliness has been my loneliness; their poverty I have endured; their wasted days have
been my own. Even their desolate islands, their deserts,
and their forests have been mine to tread.

Unlike them I cannot speak with tongues, unlike them I
cannot even adequately describe my wanderings. Yet for a

brief interval as a teacher and lecturer I have been allowed to act as their interpreter and because no man
knows what vibrations he sets in motion in his lifetime, I
am content. Has not Saint Paul said that there are many
kinds of voices in the world and none is without significa-
tion?

At a university's opening exercises, in this era of carefully directed advising, in this day of grueling college
board examinations and aptitude tests, I have been
permitted just once to cry out to our herded youngsters:
"Wait, forget the Dean of Admissions who, if I came today
in youth before him might not have permitted me to regis-
ter; be wary of our dubious advice. Freshmen, sopho-
mores, with the gift of youth upon you, do not be prematurely withered up by us. Are you uncertain about your
destiny? Take heart, in middle age I am still seeking my
true calling. I was born a stranger. Perhaps some of you
are strangers too." I said this, and much more besides, and
was blushing for my impulsive folly, when students I did
not know began to invade my office or come up to speak to
me on the campus.

I learned in that moment just how much we have lost in
our inability to communicate across the generations. I
learned how deep, how wrapped in mummy cloth, re-
pressed, long buried, lies in our minds the darkest wound
that time has given us. The men of my profession speak
frequently of the physical scars of evolution. They mean
by this that we carry in our bodies evidence of the long
way we have traveled. There is written even in our bones
the many passages at arms upon the road. To the student
of the past we are as scarred and ragged as old battle
flags. We drag with us into the future the tatters of defeat
as well as of victory: impulses of deep-buried animal
aggression, unconscious midbrain rivalries that hurl us into
senseless accidents upon the road, even as nations, which,
after all, are but a few men magnified, similarly destroy

themselves upon the even more dangerous roads of history.

From the standpoint of the hungry spirit, however, humanity has suffered an even greater wound—the ability of the mind to extend itself across a duration greater than the capacity of mortal flesh to endure. It is part of the burden of all these hungry creative voices that assail us, as it is part of the unsophisticated but equally hungry students who followed me to my office, not because of me but because of some chord in their minds which I must have momentarily and unconsciously plucked. It is, in brief, the wound of time—that genius of man, which, as Emerson long ago remarked, "is a continuation of the power that made him and that has not done making him."

When man acquired "otherness," when he left the safe confines of the instinctive world of animals, he became conscious of his own mortality. Locked in this evolution-scarred and wounded body was a mind which needed only the stimulus of knowledge to reach across the eons of the past or hurl itself upon the future. Has it occurred to us sufficiently that it is part of the continuing growth of this mind that it may desire to be lost—lost among whalebones in the farthest seas, in that great book of which its author, Melville, wrote, "a polar wind blows through it," lost among the instinctive villainies of insects in the parched field where Henri Fabre labored, lost with St.-Exupéry amidst the crevasses and thin air of the high Andes, down which the first airmail pilots drifted to their deaths? Are these great visions and insights matter for one lifetime that we must needs compress them at twenty, safely controlled, into the little rivulet of a single profession—the powers exorcised, the magnificent torrent siphoned into the safe container of a single life—this mind which, mortal and encased in flesh, would contain the past and seek to devour eternity? "As the dead man is spiritualized . . . ," remarks Thoreau, "so the imagination requires a long range.

It is the faculty of the poet to see present things as if also past and future; as if distant or universally significant." The evolutionary wound we bear has been the creation of a thing abstracted out of time yet trapped within it: the mind, by chance distorted, locked into a white-ribbed cage which effervesces into air the moment it approaches wisdom.

These are our students and ourselves, sticks of fragile calcium, little sacs of watery humors that dry away in too much heat or turn crystalline with cold; no great thing, really, if the thermometer is to be our gauge, or the small clerk stool of a single profession is to measure life. Rather, "What shall be grand in thee," wrote Melville searching his far-flung waters of memory, "must needs be plucked at from the skies, and dived for in the deep, and featured in the unbodied air."

VIII

Not all men possess such stamina, not all sustain such flights of intellect, but each of us should be aware that they exist. It is important that creature comfort does not dull the mind to somnolence. "The more an organism learns," John Dewey wrote, "the more it has to learn in order to keep itself going." This acceleration, so well documented in the history of civilization, is perceived by Dewey to characterize inflexibly the life of the individual. As an archaeologist, however, gazing from the air upon the faint outlines of the neolithic hill forts still visible upon the English downs or, similarly, upon the monoliths of Stonehenge, I am aware of something other than the geometric extension of power, whether in a civilization or a man.

There comes a time when the thistles spring up over man's ruins with a sense of relief. It is as though the wasting away of power through time had brought with it the retreat of something shadowy and not untouched with evil. The tiny incremental thoughts of men tend to congeal in vast fabrics, from gladiatorial coliseums to skyscrapers, and then mutely demand release. In the end the mind rejects the hewn stone and rusting iron it has used as the visible expression of its inner dream. Instead it asks release for new casts at eternity, new opportunities to confine the uncapturable and elusive gods.

It is one of the true functions of education to teach, in just this figurative way, the pure recompense of observing sunlight and the nodding weed wash over our own individual years and ruins. Joy was there and lingers in the grasses, the black wrong lies forever buried, and the tortured mind may seek its peace. Here all is open to the sun. The youthful rebel lies down with his double, the successful man. Or the reverse—who is to judge?

I, who endured the solitude of an ice age in my youth, remember now the yellow buttercups of the only picnic I was ever taken on in kindergarten. There are other truths than those contained in laboratory burners, on blackboards, or in test tubes. With the careful suppressions of age the buttercups grow clearer in my memory year by year. I am trying to write honestly from my own experience. I am trying to say that buttercups, a mastodon tooth, a giant snail, and a rolling Elizabethan line are a part of my own ruins over which the weeds grow tall.

I have not paused there in many years, but the light grows long in retrospect, and I have peace because I am released from pain. I know not how, yet I know also that I have been in some degree created by those lost objects in the grass. We are in truth sculptors in snow, we educators, but, thank God, we are sometimes aided by that wild fitfulness which is called "hazard," "contingency," and the indeterminacy which Dewey labeled "thinking." If the mind is indigenous and integral to nature itself in its unfolding, and operates in nature's ways and under nature's laws, we must seek to understand this creative aspect of nature in its implications for the human mind. I have tried, therefore, to point out that the natural laws of the mind include an emergent novelty with which education has to cope and elaborate for its best and fullest realization.

In Bimini, on the old Spanish Main, a black girl once said to me, "Those as hunts treasure must go alone, at night, and when they find it they have to leave a little of their blood behind them."

I have never heard a finer, cleaner estimate of the price of wisdom. I wrote it down at once under a sea lamp, like the belated pirate I was, for the girl had given me unknowingly the latitude and longitude of a treasure—a treasure more valuable than all the aptitude tests of this age.

14

THE BROWN WASPS

THERE is a corner in the waiting room of one of the great Eastern stations where women never sit. It is always in the shadow and overhung by rows of lockers. It is, however, always frequented—not so much by genuine travelers as by the dying. It is here that a certain element of the abandoned poor seeks a refuge out of the weather, clinging for a few hours longer to the city that has fathered them. In a precisely similar manner I have seen, on a sunny day in midwinter, a few old brown wasps creep slowly over an abandoned wasp nest in a thicket. Numbed and forgetful and frost-blackened, the hum of the spring hive still resounded faintly in their sodden tissues. Then the temperature would fall and they would drop away into the white oblivion of the snow. Here in the station it is in no way different save that the city is busy in its snows. But the old ones cling to their seats as though these were symbolic and could not be given up. Now and then they sleep, their gray old heads resting with painful awkwardness on the backs of the benches.

Also they are not at rest. For an hour they may sleep in the gasping exhaustion of the ill-nourished and aged who have to walk in the night. Then a policeman comes by on his round and nudges them upright.

"You can't sleep here," he growls.

A strange ritual then begins. An old man is difficult to waken. After a muttered conversation the policeman presses a coin into his hand and passes fiercely along the benches prodding and gesturing toward the door. In his wake, like birds rising and settling behind the passage of a farmer through a cornfield, the men totter up, move a few paces, and subside once more upon the benches.

One man, after a slight, apologetic lurch, does not move at all. Tubercularly thin, he sleeps on steadily. The policeman does not look back. To him, too, this has become a ritual. He will not have to notice it again officially for another hour.

Once in a while one of the sleepers will not awake. Like the brown wasps, he will have had his wish to die in the great droning center of the hive rather than in some lonely room. It is not so bad here with the shuffle of footsteps and the knowledge that there are others who share the bad luck of the world. There are also the whistles and the sounds of everyone, everyone in the world, starting on journeys. Amidst so many journeys somebody is bound to come out all right. Somebody.

Maybe it was on a like thought that the brown wasps fell away from the old paper nest in the thicket. You hold till the last, even if it is only to a public seat in a railroad station. You want your place in the hive more than you want a room or a place where the aged can be eased gently out of the way. It is the place that matters, the place at the heart of things. It is life that you want, that bruises your gray old head with the hard chairs; a man has a right to his place.

But sometimes the place is lost in the years behind us. Or sometimes it is a thing of air, a kind of vaporous distortion above a heap of rubble. We cling to a time and a place because without them man is lost, not only man but life. This is why the voices, real or unreal, which speak from the floating trumpets at spiritualist seances are so unnerving. They are voices out of nowhere whose only reality lies in their ability to stir the memory of a living person with some fragment of the past. Before the medium's cabinet both the dead and the living revolve endlessly about an episode, a place, an event that has already been engulfed by time.

This feeling runs deep in life; it brings stray cats running over endless miles, and birds homing from the ends of the earth. It is as though all living creatures, and particularly the more intelligent, can survive only by fixing or transforming a bit of time into space or by securing a bit of space with its objects immortalized and made permanent in time. For example, I once saw, on a flower pot in my own living room, the efforts of a field mouse to build a remembered field. I have lived to see this episode repeated in a thousand guises, and since I have spent a large portion of my life in the shade of a nonexistent tree I think I am entitled to speak for the field mouse.

One day as I cut across the field which at that time extended on one side of our suburban shopping center, I found a giant slug feeding from a runnel of pink ice cream in an abandoned Dixie cup. I could see his eyes telescope and protrude in a kind of dim uncertain ecstasy as his dark body bunched and elongated in the curve of the cup. Then, as I stood there at the edge of the concrete, contemplating the slug, I began to realize it was like standing on a shore where a different type of life creeps up and fumbles tentatively among the rocks and sea wrack. It knows its place and will only creep so far until something changes. Little by little as I stood there I began to see more of this shore that surrounds the place of man. I looked with sudden care and attention at things I had been running over thoughtlessly for years. I even waded out a short way into the grass and the wild-rose thickets to see more. A huge black-belted bee went droning by and there were some indistinct scurryings in the underbrush.

Then I came to a sign which informed me that this field was to be the site of a new Wanamaker suburban store. Thousands of obscure lives were about to perish, the spores of puffballs would go smoking off to new fields, and the bodies of little white-footed mice would be crunched under the inexorable wheels of the bulldozers. Life disappears or modifies its appearances so fast that everything takes on an aspect of illusion—a momentary fizzing and boiling with smoke rings, like pouring dissident chemicals into a retort. Here man was advancing, but in a few years his plaster and bricks would be disappearing once more into the insatiable maw of the clover. Being of an archaeological cast of mind, I thought of this fact with an obscure sense of satisfaction and waded back through the rose thickets to the concrete parking lot. As I did so, a mouse scurried ahead of me, frightened of my steps if not of that ominous Wanamaker sign. I saw him vanish in the general direction of my apartment house, his little body quivering with fear in the great open sun on the blazing concrete. Blinded and confused, he was running straight away from his field. In another week scores would follow him.

I forgot the episode then and went home to the quiet of my living room. It was not until a week later, letting myself into the apartment, that I realized I had a visitor. I am fond of plants and had several ferns standing on the floor in pots to avoid the noon glare by the south window.

As I snapped on the light and glanced carelessly around the room, I saw a little heap of earth on the carpet and a scrabble of pebbles that had been kicked merrily over the edge of one of the flower pots. To my astonishment I discovered a full-fledged burrow delving downward among the fern roots. I waited silently. The creature who had made the burrow did not appear. I remembered the wild field then, and the flight of the mice. No house mouse, no *Mus domesticus,* had kicked up this little heap of earth or sought refuge under a fern root in a flower pot. I thought of the desperate little creature I had seen fleeing from the wild-rose thicket. Through intricacies of pipes and attics, he, or one of his fellows, had climbed to this high green solitary room. I could visualize what had occurred. He had an image in his head, a world of seed pods and quiet, of green sheltering leaves in the dim light among the weed stems. It was the only world he knew and it was gone.

Somehow in his flight he had found his way to this room with drawn shades where no one would come till nightfall. And here he had smelled green leaves and run quickly up the flower pot to dabble his paws in common earth. He had even struggled half the afternoon to carry his burrow deeper and had failed. I examined the hole, but no whiskered twitching face appeared. He was gone. I gathered up the earth and refilled the burrow. I did not expect to find traces of him again.

Yet for three nights thereafter I came home to the darkened room and my ferns to find the dirt kicked gaily about the rug and the burrow reopened, though I was never able to catch the field mouse within it. I dropped a little food about the mouth of the burrow, but it was never touched. I looked under beds or sat reading with one ear cocked for rustlings in the ferns. It was all in vain; I never saw him. Probably he ended in a trap in some other tenant's room.

But before he disappeared I had come to look hopefully for his evening burrow. About my ferns there had begun to linger the insubstantial vapor of an autumn field, the distilled essence, as it were, of a mouse brain in exile from its home. It was a small dream, like our dreams, carried a long and weary journey along pipes and through spider webs, past holes over which loomed the shadows of waiting cats, and finally, desperately, into this room where he had played in the shuttered daylight for an hour among the green ferns on the floor. Every day these invisible dreams pass us on the street, or rise from beneath our feet, or look out upon us from beneath a bush.

Some years ago the old elevated railway in Philadelphia was torn down and replaced by a subway system. This ancient El with its barnlike stations containing nut-vending machines and scattered food scraps had, for generations, been the favorite feeding ground of flocks of pigeons, generally one flock to a station along the route of the El. Hundreds of pigeons were dependent upon the system. They flapped in and out of its stanchions and steel work or gathered in watchful little audiences about the feet of anyone who rattled the peanut-vending machines. They even watched people who jingled change in their hands, and prospected for food under the feet of the crowds who gathered between trains. Probably very few among the waiting people who tossed a crumb to an eager pigeon realized that this El was like a food-bearing river, and that the life which haunted its banks was dependent upon the running of the trains with their human freight.

I saw the river stop.

The time came when the underground tubes were ready; the traffic was transferred to a realm unreachable by pigeons. It was like a great river subsiding suddenly into desert sands. For a day, for two days, pigeons continued to circle over the El or stand close to the red vending machines. They were patient birds, and surely this great river which had flowed through the lives of unnumbered generations was merely suffering from some momentary drought.

They listened for the familiar vibrations that had always heralded an approaching train; they flapped hopefully about the head of an occasional workman walking along the steel runways. They passed from one empty station to another, all the while growing hungrier. Finally they flew away.

I thought I had seen the last of them about the El, but there was a revival and it provided a curious instance of the memory of living things for a way of life or a locality that has long been cherished. Some weeks after the El was abandoned workmen began to tear it down. I went to work every morning by one particular station, and the time came when the demolition crews reached this spot. Acetylene torches showered passers-by with sparks, pneumatic drills hammered at the base of the structure, and a blind man who, like the pigeons, had clung with his cup to a stairway leading to the change booth, was forced to give up his place.

It was then, strangely, momentarily, one morning that I witnessed the return of a little band of the familiar pigeons. I even recognized one or two members of the flock that had lived around this particular station before they were dispersed into the streets. They flew bravely in and out among the sparks and the hammers and the shouting workmen. They had returned—and they had returned because the hubbub of the wreckers had convinced them that the river was about to flow once more. For several hours they flapped in and out through the empty windows, nodding their heads and watching the fall of girders with attentive little eyes. By the following morning the station was reduced to some burned-off stanchions in the street. My bird friends had gone. It was plain, however, that they retained a memory for an insubstantial structure now compounded of air and time. Even the blind man clung to it. Someone had provided him with a chair, and he sat at the same corner staring sightlessly at an invisible stairway where, so far as he was concerned, the crowds were still ascending to the trains.

I have said my life has been passed in the shade of a nonexistent tree, so that such sights do not offend me. Prematurely I am one of the brown wasps and I often sit with them in the great droning hive of the station, dreaming sometimes of a certain tree. It was planted sixty years ago by a boy with a bucket and a toy spade in a little Nebraska town. That boy was myself. It was a cottonwood sapling and the boy remembered it because of some words spoken by his father and because everyone died or moved away who was supposed to wait and grow old under its shade. The boy was passed from hand to hand, but the tree for some intangible reason had taken root in his mind. It was under its branches that he sheltered; it was from this tree that his memories, which are my memories, led away into the world.

After sixty years the mood of the brown wasps grows heavier upon one. During a long inward struggle I thought it would do me good to go and look upon that actual tree. I found a rational excuse in which to clothe this madness. I purchased a ticket and at the end of two thousand miles I walked another mile to an address that was still the same. The house had not been altered.

I came close to the white picket fence and reluctantly, with great effort, looked down the long vista of the yard. There was nothing there to see. For sixty years that cottonwood had been growing in my mind. Season by season its seeds had been floating farther on the hot prairie winds. We had planted it lovingly there, my father and I, because he had a great hunger for soil and live things growing, and because none of these things had long been ours to protect. We had planted the little sapling and watered it faithfully, and I remembered that I had run out with my small bucket to drench its roots the day we moved away.

And all the years since it had been growing in my mind, a huge tree that somehow stood for my father and the love I bore him. I took a grasp on the picket fence and forced myself to look again.

A boy with the hard bird eye of youth pedaled a tricycle slowly up beside me.

"What'cha lookin' at?" he asked curiously.

"A tree," I said.

"What for?" he said.

"It isn't there," I said, to myself mostly, and began to walk away at a pace just slow enough not to seem to be running.

"What isn't there?" the boy asked. I didn't answer. It was obvious I was attached by a thread to a thing that had never been there, or certainly not for long. Something that had to be held in the air, or sustained in the mind, because it was part of my orientation in the universe and I could not survive without it. There was more than an animal's attachment to a place. There was something else, the attachment of the spirit to a grouping of events in time; it was part of our mortality.

So I had come home at last, driven by a memory in the brain as surely as the field mouse who had delved long ago into my flower pot or the pigeons flying forever amidst the rattle of nut-vending machines. These, the burrow under the greenery in my living room and the red-bellied bowls of peanuts now hovering in midair in the minds of pigeons, were all part of an elusive world that existed nowhere and yet everywhere. I looked once at the real world about me while the persistent boy pedaled at my heels.

It was without meaning, though my feet took a remembered path. In sixty years the house and street had rotted out of my mind. But the tree, the tree that no longer was, that had perished in its first season, bloomed on in my individual mind, unblemished as my father's words. "We'll plant a tree here, son, and we're not going to move any more. And when you're an old, old man you can sit under it and think how we planted it here, you and me, together."

I began to outpace the boy on the tricycle.

"Do you live here, Mister?" he shouted after me suspiciously. I took a firm grasp on airy nothing—to be precise, on the bole of a great tree. "I do," I said. I spoke for myself, one field mouse, and several pigeons. We were all out of touch but somehow permanent. It was the world that had changed.

BIBLIOGRAPHY

AIKEN, CONRAD. *Collected Poems*. New York: Oxford University Press, 1953.

ARVIN, NEWTON. *Herman Melville: A Critical Biography*. New York: Viking, Compass Books, 1957.

BRANDON, S. G. F. *History, Time and Deity*. New York: Barnes and Noble, 1965.

COTTRELL, LEONARD. *Lost Cities*. New York: Rinehart, 1957.

CRUTTWELL, PATRICK. *The Shakespearian Moment*. New York: Random House, 1959.

DE LA MARE, WALTER. *Ding Dong Bell*. London: Faber & Faber, 1924.

DEWEY, JOHN. *The Quest for Certainty*. New York: Putnam, Capricorn Edition, 1960.

———. *Experience and Nature*. 2nd ed. New York: Dover Publications, 1958.

DODDS, E. R. *Pagan and Christian in an Age of Anxiety.* New York: Cambridge University Press, 1965.

EISELEY, LOREN. *Darwin's Century.* New York: Doubleday, 1958.

FLACELIERE, ROBERT. *Greek Oracles.* London: Elek Books, 1965.

GONEIM, M. ZAKARIA. *The Lost Pyramid.* New York: Rinehart, 1956.

HEIM, KARL. *The Transformation of the Scientific World View.* London: SCM Press Ltd., 1953.

JARRELL, RANDALL. "On Preparing to Read Kipling," *American Scholar,* 31 (1962), 220-235.

KUBIE, LAWRENCE. *Neurotic Distortion of the Creative Process.* Lawrence, Kansas: University of Kansas Press, 1958.

MACHEN, ARTHUR. *The Hill of Dreams.* New York: Alfred A. Knopf, 1927.

MANUEL, FRANK E. *Shapes of Philosophical History.* Stanford, Calif.: Stanford University Press, 1965.

MATTHEWS, KENNETH B., JR. *Cities in the Sand: Leptis Magna and Sabratha in Roman Africa.* Philadelphia: University of Pennsylvania Press, 1957.

MEDAWAR, P. B. *The Future of Man.* New York: Mentor Books, 1961.

NEWSOM, CARROLL. *A University President Speaks Out.* New York: Harper & Row, 1961.

NICOLSON, MARJORIE HOPE. *Mountain Gloom and Mountain Glory.* New York: W. W. Norton, The Norton Library, 1963.

OLSON, CHARLES. *Call Me Ishmael: A Study of Melville.* New York: Grove Press, 1947.

PETITCLERC, DENNE. Interview with Robert Hofstadter, *San Francisco Chronicle,* November 4, 1961, p. 4.

RIEFF, PHILIP. *Freud: The Mind of the Moralist.* New York: Doubleday Anchor Books, 1961.

ROBERTSON, JOHN (ed.). *The Philosophical Works of Francis Bacon.* 1 vol. ed. London: George Routledge & Sons, 1905.

ROKEACH, MILTON. "The Pursuit of the Creative Process," in *The Creative Organization,* Gary A. Steiner (ed.), Glencoe, Ill.: The Free Press, 1962.

ROSTAND, JEAN. *The Substance of Man.* New York: Doubleday, 1962.

SCHNEER, CECIL J. *The Search for Order.* New York: Harper & Row, 1960.

THOMPSON, RUTH D'ARCY. *D'Arcy Wentworth Thompson: The Scholar-Naturalist,* 1860-1948. London: Oxford University Press, 1958.

THOREAU, HENRY DAVID. *A Writer's Journal.* Edited by Laurence Stapleton. New York: Dover Publications, 1960.

VAN DOREN, MARK. *Nathaniel Hawthorne: A Critical Biography.* New York: Viking, Compass Books, 1957.

WARD, F. KINGDON. *Modern Exploration.* London: Jonathan Cape, 1945.

WEIGAL, ARTHUR E. P. *Travels in the Upper Egyptian Deserts.* London: William Blackwood and Sons, 1913.

WILLIAMS, CHARLES. *Bacon.* New York: Harper & Brothers [n.d.].

ABOUT THE AUTHOR

LOREN EISELEY, Benjamin Franklin Professor of Anthropology and the History of Science at the University of Pennsylvania in Philadelphia, spent his boyhood among the salt flats and sunflower forests of eastern Nebraska and the high plains beyond the 99th meridian. Author of several award-winning books, Dr. Eiseley is widely known both as a naturalist and as a humanist. His work is represented in many anthologies of English prose, and he has the distinction of being an elected member of the National Institute of Arts and Letters. Dr. Eiseley has lectured at leading institutions of learning throughout the United States and has been the recipient of many honorary degrees. He serves on the Advisory Board to the National Parks system and is a past Provost of the University of Pennsylvania, as well as being Curator of Early Man in the University Museum.